Sunday Adelaja

Life is an Opportunity

Sunday Adelaja

Life is an Opportunity
©2016
ISBN 978-617-7394-06-7

London, United Kingdom
All rights reserved
www.dsa.com

Cover design by Olexandr Bondaruk

© DSA
Life is an Opportunity

London, United Kingdom

TABLE OF CONTENTS

PREFACE

Every day God packages opportunity parcels on our way. Life itself is full of parcels of gifts. Every new dawn brings thousands of parcels of gifts packaged in every day of our lives.

It is, therefore, alarming, to come to the realisation that most people are not even aware of this. Worst still, many erroneously believe that there are no opportunities in life. Where then is the confusion? What is happening? Where is the big difference or dichotomy between God and his perspective to life and the perspective of his people?

In this book, I have endeavoured to painstakingly write out in details all you need to know about taking advantage of opportunities. As someone who while growing up as a child in Africa used to believe that life lacks opportunities, I know exactly how most people without opportunities feel. That is why I know how to help people like this.

Even Though I had written this book originally in Russian language, I decided to release it in English as part of my 50 book birthday gift celebration. It is my prayer that you will not let yourself remain where life has placed you, but that you will rise up to take the bull by the horn and go for all the opportunities that God has in mind for you.

For the Love of God, Church and Nation
Dr. Sunday Adelaja.

INTRODUCTION

Most people spend their lives believing an opportunity will appear, almost mystically, and that somehow things will start to improve in their lives. This cliché is known as "waiting for the big break". The fundamental flaw in this belief is the word 'waiting'. The condition of your finances, relationships, career, business or health are always under scrutiny, yet you wait and hope for the best (to come to you). Something tells you there must be more to life than this and you know you can do better, but yet you are failing to identify the opportunity to create the solutions to affect any changes in your life.

This is not another self-help book; it is a practical guide on how to seize opportunities. If you take this book as an opportunity in itself and diligently engage in the exercises and apply the truths to your lifestyle, you will achieve success and the joy of prosperity.

Once upon a time there lived a man named Ivan Spade. His life was lacking in variety and interest: he would go to the job he hated every day, to maintain a salary that was not sufficient for the things he wanted.

His personal life was even worse: he constantly quarrelled with his wife, whom he had never loved and had no real friendship. He did not have any real friends or close relationships with anyone.

Ivan had a neighbour who had everything Ivan wanted and dreamed of in life. His neighbour loved his wife – a beautiful blond, exactly Ivan's type of lady. His neighbour owned and lived in a beautiful home with a garage and swimming pool, he owned and drove a top-of-the-range-car. His neighbour had lots of friends who regularly visited him and his wife in their home. His neighbour and his friend enjoyed each other's company as they joked and laughed out loud.

Every morning as Ivan went to work, he would envy his neighbour, and pray to God to give him everything like his neighbour. Day by day life went on and nothing changed; eventually Ivan retired, grew old and died.

Note: Ivan illustrates the behaviour of many people in terms of what they want in life – believing their wishes and desires will magically appear in their lives without taking any action to make it happen. Do you know anyone like that?

In heaven Ivan appeared before God, and God told him: *"Ivan, you have lived a normal, honest life, so*

I give you the key to the door. Go on, open it". Ivan went down a long corridor, in which there were many doors. One of them had a sign which said *"For Ivan Spade".* He was surprised to see a door just for him; when he opened the door he was blown away. Inside was the beautiful house he had always dreamed of, with a swimming pool. He also saw his dream car, in his favourite colour. There was an irresistible lady to whom he was instantly attracted, and should/would have been his wife. He saw himself relaxing with his lady and friends in this beautiful house. Ivan was furious when he saw all these wonderful things packaged for him.

He turned to God and cried out, "But why? I prayed to you every day of my life on earth for all of these beautiful things. Why didn't you answer my prayers? Why did I have to live a life of sadness and poverty? Why couldn't you give me this life on earth?" God replied, *"Do you remember that time you were on the bus, and a pretty girl sat next to you? You were looking at her in admiration but you got scared. You did not take the courage to speak to her; you were both made for each other and would have loved each other forever. Do you remember how your colleague offered you an online business proposition, but you thought it was a scam? You did not even bother to research the business offering before you said no, you were afraid. This business would have been perfect for you, and it would have been lucrative and you would have been successful at it. The income and opportunities from the business would have enabled you to buy everything you wanted and live your dream life. Do you remember the night when your classmate came and asked for help? Although you could help, you were too consumed by yourself and did not lend a hand. You did not care about your friend's plight. He could have been your most loyal friend and with your friendship with him, you would have made a host of more good friends. I gave you everything you asked for and more, I just didn't indicate with obvious signs 'for Ivan Spade'."*

Most people go through life seeking opportunities that will improve their lives. Opportunities in the areas of finance, family happiness, inner peace, health and success are all common in any society. We want a lot a lot in life but often achieve little; we become frustrated with no hope of solace.

Where are all these opportunities hidden, you ask? Where do I find them and how can I achieve the fortune of success? I want to challenge you today, to know and believe that you already have the ability to hold your own and be a success.

By the very act of reading this book you are creating an opportunity for yourself today, embarking on the ladder to the top. The fact that you know about the existence of a loving God who hears you and cares about you is also an opportunity. Seize the opportunity of the knowledge of a loving God to enlarge your coast. The fact that books like this are published and accessible to more people is also an opportunity – continue to develop this opportunity until you get what you want. Some people will take this opportunity and use it and others will just let it pass them by. What are you going to do?

In this book, we will focus on opportunities. This is a book with practical exercises and explanations of how to identify opportunities and use these opportunities to achieve happiness, success, joy, prosperity and much more. Throughout this book you will learn how to seize opportunities to your benefit. By learning, understanding and using the chances present in this life, you will be pleasantly surprised by how much your life and your environment will transform for the better.

Remember, it is better to take charge of your life than to wait for fate to take care of you.

Most people spend their lives believing an opportunity will appear, almost mystically, and that somehow things will start to improve in their lives. This cliché is known as "waiting for the big break". The fundamental flaw in this belief is the word 'waiting'. The condition of your finances, relationships, career, business or health are always under scrutiny, yet you wait and hope for the best (to come to you). Something tells you there must be more to life than this and you know you can do better, but yet you are failing to identify the opportunity to create the solutions to affect any changes in your life.

This is not another self-help book; it is a practical guide on how to seize opportunities. If you take this book as an opportunity in itself and diligently engage in the exercises and apply the truths to your lifestyle, you will achieve success and the joy of prosperity.

Once upon a time there lived a man named Ivan Spade. His life was lacking in variety and interest: he would go to the job he hated every day, to maintain a salary that was not sufficient for the things he wanted. His personal life was even worse: he constantly quarrelled with his wife, whom he had never loved and had no real friendship. He did not have any real friends or close relationships with anyone.

Ivan had a neighbour who had everything Ivan wanted and dreamed of in life. His neighbour loved his wife – a beautiful blond, exactly Ivan's type of lady. His neighbour owned and lived in a beautiful home with a garage and swimming pool, he owned and drove a top-of-the-range-car. His neighbour had lots of friends who regularly visited him and his wife in their home. His neighbour and his friend enjoyed each other's company as they joked and laughed out loud.

Every morning as Ivan went to work, he would envy his neighbour, and pray to God to give him everything like his neighbour. Day by day life went on and nothing changed; eventually Ivan retired, grew old and died.

Note: Ivan illustrates the behaviour of many people in terms of what they want in life – believing their wishes and desires will magically appear in their lives without taking any action to make it happen. Do you know anyone like that?

In heaven Ivan appeared before God, and God told him: *"Ivan, you have lived a normal, honest life, so I give you the key to the door. Go on, open it"*. Ivan went down a long corridor, in which there were many doors. One of them had a sign which said *"For Ivan Spade"*. He was surprised to see a door just for him; when he opened the door he was blown away. Inside was the beautiful house he had always dreamed of, with a swimming pool. He also saw his dream car, in his favourite colour. There was an irresistible lady to whom he was instantly attracted, and should/would have been his wife. He saw himself relaxing with his lady and friends in this beautiful house. Ivan was furious when he saw all these wonderful things packaged for him.

He turned to God and cried out, "But why? I prayed to you every day of my life on earth for all of these beautiful things. Why didn't you answer my prayers? Why did I have to live a life of sadness and poverty? Why couldn't you give me this life on earth?" God replied, *"Do you remember that time you were on the bus, and a pretty girl sat next to you? You were looking at her in admiration but you got scared. You did not take the courage to speak to her; you were both made for each other and would have loved each other forever. Do you remember how your colleague offered you an online business proposition, but you thought it was a scam? You did not even bother to research the business offering before you said no, you were afraid. This business would have been perfect for you, and it would have been lucrative and you would have been successful at it. The income and opportunities from the business would have enabled you to buy everything you wanted and live your dream life. Do you remember the night when your classmate came and asked for help?*

Although you could help, you were too consumed by yourself and did not lend a hand. You did not care about your friend's plight. He could have been your most loyal friend and with your friendship with him, you would have made a host of more good friends. I gave you everything you asked for and more, I just didn't indicate with obvious signs 'for Ivan Spade'."

Most people go through life seeking opportunities that will improve their lives. Opportunities in the areas of finance, family happiness, inner peace, health and success are all common in any society. We want a lot a lot in life but often achieve little; we become frustrated with no hope of solace.

Where are all these opportunities hidden, you ask? Where do I find them and how can I achieve the fortune of success? I want to challenge you today, to know and believe that you already have the ability to hold your own and be a success.

By the very act of reading this book you are creating an opportunity for yourself today, embarking on the ladder to the top. The fact that you know about the existence of a loving God who hears you and cares about you is also an opportunity. Seize the opportunity of the knowledge of a loving God to enlarge your coast. The fact that books like this are published and accessible to more people is also an opportunity – continue to develop this opportunity until you get what you want. Some people will take this opportunity and use it and others will just let it pass them by. What are you going to do?

In this book, we will focus on opportunities. This is a book with practical exercises and explanations of how to identify opportunities and use these opportunities to achieve happiness, success, joy, prosperity and much more. Throughout this book you will learn how to seize opportunities to your benefit. By learning, understanding and using the chances present in this life, you will be pleasantly surprised by how much your life and your environment will transform for the better.

Remember, it is better to take charge of your life than to wait for fate to take care of you.

Chapter 1

LIFE IS FULL
OF OPPORTUNITIES

Chapter 1
LIFE IS FULL
OF OPPORTUNITIES

Thomas Alva Edison was an American inventor and businessman. He developed many devices that greatly influenced life around the world, including the phonograph, the motion picture camera, and the long-lasting, practical electric light bulb. One of his triumphs – the electric light bulb – changed the lives of many people in the late 19th century. It caused a revolution with the appearance of the lamp in 1879. Edison's system of production and consumption of electric energy could be considered for an urban area, and even a whole city. This inventor did not just stop at creating the product, he discovered ways for it to be accessible to all and made the light bulb cheap and easy to use – so that lighting candles became a luxury. Edison's vision for electric energy in urban areas and cities may have developed from the impact of light both on safety and the prospect of better living conditions it represents. These same reasons prompted most of his inventions.

Thomas Edison's great grandfather was faithful to the British crown during the American Revolution when he was posted to serve in Canada. His son also fought as a British citizen during the Anglo-American War of 1812. Edison would have remained in Canada if his father had not tried to conspire with the ranks of local conspirators, who spoke against the British. After the failure of the conspiracy Samuel Edison, along with his young wife, a descendant of a family of American expats, went into hiding. Following the events of the war the family had no choice but to risk it all and go to the United States. If destiny had treated Thomas Edison's great grandparents differently they would have never settled in America. In the late 1830s, Sam Edison constantly feared for his life, trying not to reveal the truth about his past in the British Empire – then the enemy of the American people. He settled in the town of Milan, Ohio with his family.

On February 11th 1847 the Edison family welcomed their seventh child of nine (three had died in infancy), and they named him Thomas Alva Edison. By the time Thomas was seven, the agricultural state of Ohio started to encounter problems with its infrastructure. The railway connecting Detroit to

Canada passed through Milan, and the town began to decay rapidly. Sam took his family to the nearby state of Michigan and the city of Port Huron, located on the shore of the lake, in an attempt to reduce the impact and the environmental challenges they had previously faced. Edison Senior tried many things, engaging in timber trade, land speculation, farming and weaving, all to no avail.

It was around this time that Thomas Edison started showing learning difficulties. In the first grade his teacher publicly called the future genius a "brainless dullard", so his indignant mother took him out of that school. His formal education lasted only a few months and he received the rest of his education at home under the guidance of his mother. Fortunately, Thomas loved to read and unlike his peers, accustomed himself to make his own toys, not depending on his parents to buy him them. By the age of ten he had started on his list of inventions, making a miniature sawmill and a toy train.

Two years later, Edison began to earn an income by selling newspapers, books and sweets on trains. As well as gaining experience with trains which he sought out as a child, the teenager read up on the wagons of his time. He invested his spare time using his imagination to invent what was not in the books.

One of his earliest creations was the world's first weekly passenger train publication, *Grand Trunk Herald*. Edison as the sole author, editor and publisher produced it in a boxcar, which was also his print shop and adapted laboratory where he developed his inventions. The newspaper was distributed by his peers, and at the age of thirteen he was already hiring others. His publication was popular, so he used the profit from the newspaper to equip his laboratory on wheels.

In 1876 Thomas Edison opened his own laboratory in the town of Menlo Park, New Jersey – the world's first inventions factory. Dozens of companies sought Edison for solutions and by the age of forty, Edison was known not only in America but also around the world. He became the creator of the phonograph (record player), electric engine, alkaline vehicle battery and the first talking dolls. Edison was also the inventor of the original method of iron ore beneficiation and predicted the use of concrete for construction. He patented hundreds of different ideas, collaborating with the likes of Alexander Graham Bell, the Scottish-born scientist, inventor, engineer and innovator who is credited with patenting the first practical telephone.

You may well ask, what set this young man with humble beginnings to achieve such outstanding success, despite many challenges? How did this individual respond to opportunities and even create opportunities for himself? What role did factors such as time and chance play in his life? Have these questions in mind and seek answers throughout this book.

Consider this poem about life by Mother Teresa MC, the Nobel Peace Prize winner known in the Catholic Church as Saint Teresa of Calcutta, an Albanian-Indian Roman Catholic nun and missionary. She was born in Skopje, then part of the Kosovo Vilayet in the Ottoman Empire.

Life is an opportunity, benefit from it.
Life is beauty, admire it.
Life is a dream, realise it.
Life is a challenge, meet it.
Life is a duty, complete it.
Life is a game, play it.
Life is a promise, fulfil it.
Life is sorrow, overcome it.
Life is a song, sing it.
Life is a struggle, accept it.
Life is a tragedy, confront it.
Life is an adventure, dare it.
Life is luck, make it.
Life is too precious, do not destroy it.
Life is life, fight for it.

Mother Teresa.

Before we start the analysis of how to respond to opportunities, let's consider this question: what qualifies as life? First let me say this: life itself is an opportunity, a chance that is given to a person only once. Human life is not just a succession of days lived; God expects us to make this chance meaningful and not to have any regrets or to have wasted life. Nikolai Alexseyevich Ostrovsky was a Soviet socialist realist writer of Ukrainian origin. In his popular novel *How the Steel was tempered*, he writes: "The most precious thing a person owns is life. It is given to him once, and it must be lived so that he will not be in excruciating pain for his wasted years, so that his petty past will not burn his soul and that with his dying breath he could say: all my life and strength was used on the most important thing in this world." Independently, we must clearly define how we live and what we live for, seeking all the opportunities life presents.

Unfortunately, most people do not realise this until the time of their death, not appreciating the value of our one chance of life on earth. We treat life as though it will never end; we live our lives completely devoid of the responsibility to make our lives meaningful during our time on earth, believing it will last forever.

The fact is, life is not our property to own – our lives are given to us by God for a period of time and sooner or later we will have to give an account of how we lived from day to day and what we did with our given strengths, skills and talents., How did we make use of the chances received by destiny? Considering life is a gift from God, we must live it to the fullest, so our creator will pronounce us good and faithful. It is important to think about life, and remember that it is finite. The years will pass by, youthfulness will flee, the time spent in vain will not return. It is important to appreciate the life that we have been given and make good use of it. Cultivate strength in times of crisis, and be of sound mind. Search and identify the opportunities in every situation, boldly taking the steps from one opportunity to the next. We must recognise that everything that is happening in our lives is for the better. Sometimes it may seem unlikely or contrary to how you view opportunities, in that case defying our perceptions. Do not lose hope as the dead-end may turn out to be a sharp turn not to the end of life, but to the beginning of a new adventure. It has been known that the most severe disappointments often turn into new opportunities, opening the door to a brighter future.

You must regularly evaluate your life, check your habits and ask yourself questions. How am I living my life? Do I know my full worth? Do I make use of my potential? If you do not regularly evaluate your life you are likely to waste the time the creator has given us. We are on this earth for a purpose and we must take every possible step to fulfilment. We must never settle or accept mediocrity – that is what fools do. Those who have the wisdom and understanding of time make productive use of it and set plans to achieve success.

Life is an opportunity – both life and opportunity wait for no one. Look at the definition: "Opportunity is a time or set of circumstances that make it possible to do something." The definition's first reference is to "time", meaning time is of crucial importance in relation to seizing and developing opportunities. If you fail to grab something when it is available, you may lose it forever. **The opportunities you take on earth are what secure your future in eternity.** Death is a cruel reminder of this: when someone close to us dies, during the grieving period most people quietly evaluate their lives. This is especially common if the passing is of a tragic nature, i.e., an accident, or when someone suddenly dies at a tender age or in their prime. Our focus temporarily turns to the purpose of life and opportunities missed. This should be a daily focus reminding ourselves of the value we have in time and seeking the opportunities it presents.

Our life is our responsibility. We must always remember we hold the key to our success and our failure and it is in our power which key we use and which door we open. Remember the story of Ivan Spade: God has given us all and more than we can ever need, the getting or receiving is up to us. Ask yourself this question: if your life ends right now, will you be satisfied? Will you be able to account for your time on earth? Did you use your talents and treasures to your full potential? Did you seize all the opportunities available to you?

Time and Opportunity

I returned, and saw under the sun,
That the race is not to the swift,
Nor the battle to the strong, neither yet bread to the wise,
Nor yet riches to men of understanding,
Nor yet favour to men of skill;
But time and chance happeneth to them all.

Ecclesiastes 9:11

The above verse from the book of Ecclesiastes further emphasises the extent of God's grace. He has provided all our needs without prejudice. This verse ends with a key assurance that "time and chance happen to all". What is your excuse now? It clearly states everyone has an equal chance, no matter your creed, location, circumstances, family, background, abilities or anything else you may have been using as an excuse.

We have learnt that life is given to us for a period of time and life in itself is an opportunity full of possibilities. We have also learnt there are two key elements to this life: time and chance. These work together to present us with opportunities. Opportunity is presented in the existence of time and the situation in time presents us with chance. Time and opportunity are inextricable; it is our responsibility to recognise the opportunity and not miss the chances available to be fulfilled.

Whatsoever thy hand findeth to do, do it with thy might; for there is no work, nor device, nor knowledge, nor wisdom, in the grave, whither thou goest. I returned, and saw under the sun, that the race is not to the swift, nor the battle to the strong, neither yet bread to the wise, nor yet riches to men of understanding, nor yet favour to men of skill; but time and chance happeneth to them all.

Ecclesiastes 9:10-11

The above verse from Ecclesiastes further expands the importance of time and chance using work as the tool to convert these two elements. It is clear that action is required from us; it is our responsibility to take the necessary action as opportunities are presented. "Whatever thy hand finds to do, do it with thy might." Everything we do, must be done with due diligence as it is presented to us in order to actualise our God's given opportunities here on earth. Time will always present a chance for us to make use of on earth. The onus is on us to identify and make use of all that has been given. Chances come in many forms, our responsibility is to seek out the opportunities in every situation. Those who do not run, do not become successful runners. Those who do not participate cannot win. Every opportunity must be backed up with action, as only by diligent application of action can success be possible.

A diligent person will always be prepared. Remember the saying, "Prior Preparation Prevents Poor Performance". When preparation has taken place, it reduces and sometimes eliminates the potential for things to go wrong. Do anything you can turn your hand to and do it well; do not give up, be persistent in what you find to do, and then certainly you will see opportunities.

The Difference between Success and Luck

In previous paragraphs, we focused on opportunities being a matter of time and chance. Now let's move on to the difference between success and luck. Most people complain about being unlucky in life. This is manifested in different ways, starting with negative self-talk. "I am unlucky because I was born into a poor family. I was unlucky in life because there was nobody to help me, and all opportunities pass by me, that's why I can't do anything tangible."

Often we look outwards and blame anyone and everything. Our blame game is as strong as our excuses. The responsibility for our own lives is delegated especially where failure is concerned. This becomes a habit, which if left unchecked becomes the justification for being complacent and accepting our shortcomings as the norm. We must cultivate the right attitude and be able to recognise and accept that we are in charge of our lives, both in failure and success. When people are dissatisfied with their lives and do not see the opportunities in life, they often complain that they are not lucky. The misconception of success is that it just happens and it happens by dream or in the form of a fairy tale. Despite the many examples of great success, through perseverance, seizing opportunities and developing ideas against all odds, many still wait for a miracle to happen to help them achieve success.

This faulty thinking or misunderstanding is prevalent in those who believe success depends on luck. Their thought system creates the fallacy that a business person at the top of his or her profession doing very well achieved this height by luck, and on the other hand someone who is struggling and unsuccessful in business or vocation is unlucky. This mental state disconnects the individual from their responsibility to take hold of their life. Our consideration for success or failure should be based on the choices we make in progressing our calling, vocation or profession. As in the verses in Ecclesiastes, everyone on earth has been given time and chance; this includes what you are called to do and be in life. Your calling may not be to become a businessman, but you will still have a calling – it is your responsibility to discover your calling. Your calling may involve a passion, or even a burden in some situations. A burden to see change in a situation could be the driving force to lead you to success. You will be successful when you do what you are called to do. Often people fail to achieve success because they are doing what is not intended for them; they drift into one action after another without evaluating if it is their purpose or their calling. Another way to identify your calling is by evaluating your strengths: what are you good at doing? What do you do effortlessly? Or what you do with great effort but enjoy?

People brought up in western civilisations have been taught from early childhood that success **is the product of purposeful action.** They have been trained to enquire and probe for answers and no matter what the situation or need, there is always a solution. This is the principle of cause and effect; this principle can also be found in the Bible, with the correlation of sowing and reaping. You will reap (harvest), what you sow. Galatians 6:7 says "do not be deceived… for whatever a man sows, this he will also reap…" It is not possible to plant a seed of a lemon and expect an orange to grow. True success is achieved by concrete actions, intensity, effort and diligent work, converted to a goal or outcome.

Most successful people start with very little capital or in some cases in the absence of any capital at all. Do you think this is a result of luck? Successful results are preceded by purposeful actions.

Here are examples of individuals who took purposeful action and achieved success:

• **Sanford Lockwood Cluett** was an American businessman and inventor known for developing Sanforization, a process to pre-shrink woven fabrics.

This discovery brought him royalties in excess of five million dollars annually.

- **Henry Ford**, the founder of the Ford Motor Company, believed in the knowledge he possessed and proclaimed to "build the cheapest car available for anyone". He did not retreat under any circumstances, proceeding with actions to achieve his objectives. He amassed great wealth in his lifetime.

- **Anita Roddick** was a British businesswoman best known as the founder of The Body Shop. She created her cosmetics company, producing and retailing natural products that shaped ethical consumerism, out of very little.

- **Bill Gates**, one of the richest men in the world, made his fortune in the pioneering of computers and continuing innovation in technology.

- **Anthony Robbins**, an American motivational speaker, personal finance instructor and self-help author, was once completely broke and living in a small apartment, but, nevertheless, within a year changed his life so that he became a millionaire and was able to acquire a lock area of 10,000 square meters with an ocean view.

- **Aristotle Onassis**, a Turkish-born Greek shipping magnate, started his business with less than

200 dollars, with the absence of any university degree or rich relatives to help him financially. Despite this, he became one of the richest people of all time.

In order to achieve the level of success reached by these individuals you must start and start from where you are now. Take a step towards a goal and do not stop. Create, do, make a plan and take action towards the plan. You make your dream come true by putting your vision to work. "A dream written down with a DATE becomes a GOAL, a goal broken down into steps become a PLAN, a plan backed by ACTION makes your dreams come true," says American author Greg S. Reid. You must never favour idleness but instead develop yourself, increase your value and be persistent in seeking knowledge. Always raise the bar higher and make it your mission to strive to new heights and without limits. Understand that you make your own luck, that you are the creator of your failure or success and that you are at the steering wheel of your own life. Where will your drive your life? Millionaires regard the time and energy they put into their projects as investments. They understand it may not give noticeable or immediate results, but are willing to make all the necessary efforts to see the fruits of their labour come to fruition. Life gives you what you put in; nobody has ever earned a million by sitting in front of the TV or lying in bed for hours a day. If you are not fortunate to win the lottery or inherit a large fortune, then you will have to be diligent in your work to achieve the heights of success.

Success is not an accident! It is a plan put into action. Exceptions such as a lottery win or an inheritance are short lived. A person who cannot manage money or understand the principles of finance will eventually falter. Real success is the result of selfless work, plan and action, as persistent action will lead to opportunities. The key to success and opportunity is persistent action and implementation of plans. There are no short cuts, as success is not about luck; it is simply goals broken down and backed up by action.

Golden Nuggets

1. Life is a set of actions – each action gives rise to the opportunities and capabilities you need to see it through.

2. Life is an opportunity on the move – it will only stay if it is backed up by action.

3. Before time and opportunity comes, a person must take action to secure provision.

4. Success is achieved not by chance, but by an arrangement of actions that seize opportunities.

5. Real success is the result of selfless work and planned opportunities reaching fruition.

Self-Examination Test

Take this test to find out how well you are able to distinguish opportunities in your life:

1. I always take responsibility for everything that happens in my life
a) I don't know – 0 points;
b) No – 1 point;
c) More so – 3 points;
d) Yes – 4 points.

2. I want to achieve success in
a) I don't know what I need – 0 points;
b) Financial well-being – 1 point;
c) Personal business – 3 points;
d) Spiritual and personal growth – 4 points.

3. The success of my neighbour is as a result of luck
a) I agree completely – 0 points;
b) Sometimes – 1 point;
c) No – 3 points;
d) If a person is successful, it is as a result of perseverance – 4 points.

4. Being part of a team is an opportunity to sit back and let others do the work

a) I agree completely – 0 points;

b) Sometimes – 1 point;

c) No – 3 points;

d) Absolutely not – 4 points.

e)

5. I am often late for work or a meeting because I do not plan ahead

a) I agree completely – 0 points;

b) Sometimes – 1 point;

c) No – 3 points;

d) Absolutely not, I plan my time well – 4 points.

Test Results

5 Points or Lower – You depend completely on chance in order to achieve your goals. You do not aspire to make enough effort and you have relinquished control of your life and ability to achieve your goals to luck. To develop the necessary qualities and the ability to recognise and seize opportunities, it is recommended you continue to read this book thoroughly and take the practical test in each section, answering all the questions in detail to gain insight into developing a personalised plan for success.

6–10 Points – Perhaps you acknowledge the role of opportunity, but you are failing to prepare. You have neglected to do your part and fail to seize the opportunity in any given situation. Your complacency and lack of conviction is a hindrance to your success. It is recommended you carefully work this out through the remaining part of the book. Hope is not lost.

11–14 Points – Congratulations! You are an example of a successful person, who does not tolerate laxity. You desire and work to live to your full potential. All your achievements are measured with efforts. Take up this challenge; duplicate your attitude to life by encouraging and educating others. Start with those who are close to you.

Recommendations for Practical Exercises

1. These practical exercises are a prerequisite for your development, a key process for your growth in learning to maximise your life. You must take the action required in the practical exercise in order to achieve the full benefits of this book. In my many years' experience of working with people, I am aware of the lack of commitment in taking practical exercises such as this. My advice to you is to take these exercises seriously and honestly.

2. High scorers are recommended to complete the practical exercises within 24 hours of reading a chapter, as any delay in this process will equate to postponing your success.

3. It is advisable to find a quiet place to focus without distractions.

4. Reflect on the previous chapter, consider all the areas you highlighted and remember to write down your thoughts and plan of action necessary to realise your goals.

5. Ensure you plans are time-bound, set limits and a specific time frame for completing each task to achieve your goal. This will set your plans in motion and prevent delays in achieving the objectives.

6. Have someone hold you accountable for the things you plan to do, the tasks you have set. This could be a mentor, a friend or family member. It is important this person is someone you respect and value as they will be reminding and challenging you to move your plans forward.

Practical Exercises

1. What is your definition of life or how would you define life?

2. What is your definition of success?

3. In your opinion, is success the result of luck and fortune or as a result of planned and diligent action? List previous sequences of your actions that led you to success.

4. "Fate gives each person a few opportunities every day." What is your understanding of this statement? Give evidence of your answer.

5. Why should you not **just** expect a favourable time (circumstance) to come to you?

Chapter 2

WHY PEOPLE
ARE BLIND
TO OPPORTUNITIES

Chapter 2
WHY PEOPLE ARE BLIND
TO OPPORTUNITIES

A nine-year-old girl from South Africa accidentally found one of the largest diamonds in the world. It was the size of her fist. She stumbled upon it near a wide pedestrian path where hundreds of people walked daily. Attracted to the stone's unusual features, the little girl picked it up to show her father, who worked at the mine. He of course suspected it might be more than just a "pretty stone". His suspicions were correct, and after the diamond was cut and polished it was valued at over two million dollars.

It is possible that if you had walked by the same stone you would have overlooked it, as did many others who passed through this path. Diamonds in their natural form look completely different from the way they look once processed and transformed into the expensive, sparkling gems we love. This notion is the same with opportunities – they sometimes come "raw" and unrefined, requiring our curiosity and action to unlock their potential. Opportunities rarely look the way you expect them to look in appearance; it will not look like the profitable company in your dream. It is an opportunity for you to make something into a finished product; it does not come as a finished product. The businessman or woman who makes so much money from transacting various businesses started from a very different place to the one that you see and admire now. Hard work and refinement later turn them into the savvy entrepreneurs you want to emulate. Opportunities actually exist, and in abundance, yet they appear in the most unusual form and places.

Our problem is not that we were not born into that family of achievers, or that we do not live in that country with seemingly successful people, or that we received an inferior education. **The trouble is that we are not able to notice and enjoy the real opportunities God sends us daily.** Let me tell you this: LIFE IS MADE UP OF OPPORTUNITIES. By definition, an opportunity is a condition or circumstance that allows us to realise something when acted upon. **Life is a set of opportunities – the choices we make are entirely up to us.** God who created the world, including us, provides opportunities for all to benefit from. Being a loving and caring God, He considers us daily with new opportunities. He knows what we need and He gives us equal chances to take and seize the opportunities He makes available daily.

Each day is endowed with countless opportunities. It is written in scripture: "Therefore do not worry about tomorrow, for tomorrow will worry about itself. Each day has enough trouble of its own." (Matthew 6:34). Trouble in itself is full of opportunities. Take the situation of economic downturn which lead to the financial crisis of 2008. Although it was considered a troubling time, many people who lost their job and home seized the opportunity to start a business or retrain in another profession in the area of their passion or hobby. The saying, "if there is a day, there is also a chance," is true. God is the master planner as He gives each day; it is blessed with provision. He is always true to His words. We must do our part of seeking these opportunities by identifying and taking action. The mere fact that you woke up today should inform you that you have a chance; the popular saying "when there is life, there is hope" is a fact of each waking day. Everything that happens to us every day, both positive and negative, includes opportunities embedded – the only requirement is that you search them out, identify and act.

In all that we see with our eyes and hear with our ears are HIDDEN OPPORTUNITIES. Most of our ideas in which opportunities lurk will not appear in our head just out of nowhere, but will come from what we read or what we see: the Internet, people, etc. Even street signs can evoke brilliant ideas. "A wise man sees before him an immeasurable realm of possibilities; a fool considers possible only what is," said Denis Diderot, French writer, philosopher, educator and playwright who compiled the *Encyclopaedia*, a translation of the *Explanatory Dictionary of Sciences, Arts and Crafts.* Always remember that regardless of where you are, the opportunities are endless; you just need to consciously seek them and act upon each one to unlock the gem within. The Sovereign God sends opportunities to each one of us each and every day. Do you see the possibilities that life sends you every day and, most importantly, do you make use of them?

Opportunities never arrive as a finished product or beautifully packaged and ready for immediate use on a silver platter. The reason is that God wants to discourage laziness. He has gifted us all with the ability to do great exploits and only in so doing do we achieve purpose. Although God does not give us the finished product, He sends us a chance in a disguised form, hidden and concealed like the diamond in its natural form. We need to seek and search for the hidden beauty in daily opportunities He gives. We must be alert and open to discover the opportunities that exist around us and seize the moment to act.

Opportunities always come unexpectedly. Usually we think that since it is an opportunity, it will be obvious to us, but opportunities are rarely apparent and possibilities do not have a signpost to prompt us to what we must do to seize them. Opportunities often appear in the most unexpected places and we must seek to find. Our duty is to search out the opportunity in any given situation or event. We must master the art of recognising opportunities. The key to this is in believing opportunities lie in every situation, seeking them out and taking action to achieve with a set of objectives. No matter how good an advisor or friend you have, nobody can seek, find and take the actions required to unravel an opportunity for you. Even when you are directed to an opportunity the onus is still on you, the individual, to distinctively seize and birth the potential in that opportunity.

Life is full of chances even if they do not announce themselves. Suddenly, you get the idea. Unexpectedly you receive an offer. Swiftly there is an opportunity for advancement and benefit. These things may happen rapidly and you will hardly have the chance to catch your breath. The irony is that when an opportunity is not seized, no one sits you down for debriefing to show where you missed a chance in seizing an opportunity. **You may not even notice the chance if you do not wilfully set your mind and body to catch an opportunity as it becomes available.** YOU MUST PREPARE FROM YOUR CORE, YOUR INNER SELF,

IN ORDER TO GRAB OPPORTUNITIES AS THEY COME.

People who are effective are often able to notice opportunities and take swift action to become successful in life. The fact is, God sends opportunities to everyone, without bias. Your location, your gender, colour and anything else you can think of does not exclude you from His grace. The principle to convert opportunity is accessible every day and with each passing day there are treasures available to all. It is our responsibility to identify these opportunities and appropriate them. Therefore, we must be attentive to the opportunities that life gives us. Such attentiveness is characterised by the knowledge and determination that we have to succeed. It is also important to develop the habit of seeking, to catch all the chances that life initiates. We must cultivate critical thinking and analysis of every situation. The skill to focus is important in capitalising on opportunities, keeping your eye on the ball. This book could be your first aide to mastering the process of seizing opportunities. Critical thinkers are leaders; if you take any event or product, it is always the case that it is conceived first in the mind before it comes to fruition. For those who are familiar with the game of chess, you will know the value of critical thinking. This is why chess players are respected, because they learn and apply depth to their thinking prowess.

Lack of knowledge is a hindrance to seeking and identifying possibilities. You would have heard many times over the saying "knowledge is power" – this is partially true, and I say 'partially' because knowledge without action is just knowledge, it will not produce anything on its own. It is important to have knowledge of the self, at least in the sense that you know who you are and what you are capable of doing. If you can't describe your capabilities (skills) to yourself or draw a clear picture of your know-hows in your mind, and therefore do not know what you can do, you probably will not be able to have any impact when opportunities arise. Whenever you do not see new opportunities or do not know what to do next, it means that you do not have enough knowledge. **Failure to identify opportunity is an indication of lack of knowledge**. In order to succeed you must have hunger to seek knowledge and satisfy a need bigger than you.

You must develop the desire for information. Signs of a shortage of information can be seen in a person who wakes up in the morning and

- Does not know what to do

- Does not see new opportunities

- Does not have any fresh ideas; a minimum of 10–20 new ideas must be born daily.

What is the solution to this lack, you ask? Your first action to correct this situation is acquiring knowledge: start by reading. Read everything, especially in the area you need or that interests you in order to develop yourself. In other words, you need to take the time to educate yourself, learn, and research and self-study what you don't know to develop, increase and intensify your knowledge of what you already know – to acquire skills and seek knowledge where it can be found. As you enter into this process, you will find new ideas evolving in and around you. Take note: as ideas are developing in you, write them down, no matter how small they seem. Someone once said "a short pencil is better than a long memory". This is absolutely true. Don't rely on your memory alone as our memories sometimes fail us; to prevent loss of ideas, write them down. We sometimes naively convince ourselves that we don't need to write everything down, "after all I thought of it so I will remember". Too often we find ourselves forgetting a very important piece of information or idea and yet we fail to learn from previous experience and cultivate the habit of writing everything down. Do yourself a favour and get a note pad and make it your habit to write down every idea that comes to your mind. You may not have the whole picture at once or at the time it first comes to you, but steadily and surely it will all unfold. Much like a puzzle once you start right and you are persistent, the whole picture will come together to create a whole new and complete image. "You cannot solve a problem at the same level at which it originated, you need to rise above the problem up to the next level," said Albert Einstein, one of the founders of modern theoretical physics and Nobel Prize winner. If you mean to solve any problems and achieve an objective which seems unattainable, you must rise to a new level in knowledge. As you develop yourself you identify new opportunities and find ways to implement your ideas to become reality.

Golden Nuggets

1. Opportunities are everywhere and always within our reach, it is our responsibility to seek and perceive opportunities and take timely action.

2. Opportunities come as a matter of fact, they come swiftly and do not wait around. No signage, no label – much like a diamond in the rough you are the refiner of the opportunities you seize.

3. It is your responsibility to search out the opportunity in a situation. Opportunities are not biased and do not discriminate. They make themselves available and accessible to all, so whoever seizes them can grab with both hands.

4. Life provides opportunities without warning, so be prepared by acquiring knowledge, skill and understanding in your area of interest. Be ready.

5. You must cultivate an attitude to identify opportunities as they arise.

6. If you fail to acquire knowledge, you will not see opportunities as you ought to. "My people are destroyed for lack of knowledge," Hosea 4:6.

Self-Examination Test

Take this test to give you some insight on how well you are able to distinguish opportunities in your life.

1. In your own opinion, how often do you come across opportunities?
a) Almost never – 0 points;
b) Very rarely, I am one of the unlucky ones – 1 point;
c) There are a few, but not enough – 2 points;
d) My life is full of amazing possibilities, and they pop up every day! – 4 points.

2. Do you notice unusual things around you?
a) Everything around me is dull and sad – 0 points;
b) There is nothing new under the sun – 1 point;
c) Oh, if I'm not constantly busy with troubles at home and at work, then during my leisure time I sometimes find something unexpected – 2 points;
d) Yes, very often in fact – 4 points.

3. How big is your expectancy of opportunities?

a) I do not expect anything good from life – 0 points;

b) Very little – 1 point;

c) I would like to be more enthusiastic in my expectations – 3 points;

d) I live in daily anticipation of new opportunities – 4 points.

4. How do you spend your spare time?

a) I do nothing – 0 points;

b) I rest or take a nap – 1 point;

c) I work on my fitness and personal wellbeing – 3 points;

d) I try to learn something new and gain new friends – 4 points.

5. I'm interested in everything new, i.e. I'm not afraid to try an unfamiliar food or drink…

a) No, this is not me at all – 0 points;

b) I rarely try anything new food – 1 point;

c) Yes, I am willing to try new food – 2 points;

d) Yes, this is absolutely me – 4 points.

Test Results

5 Points or Lower – Your ability to identify opportunities in life is negligible. Even if an opportunity is on a silver platter for you, you will still miss it. This may be because you are not attuned to the fact that opportunities are available in every situation and that they are yours to seek without reservation. To develop a grip on the reality of life's opportunities, continue to read this book and focus on the lessons to the end. Ensure you complete the practical assignment on each chapter.

6–10 Points – You hardly notice even the most obvious opportunities in your life, you are still waiting for tangible clues to serve you the possibilities of life on a silver platter. As a result of your lethargy you are missing many chances that could launch you into your destiny. As an immediate solution, you must develop the skills to gravitate on everything that offers you a chance. It is recommended you wisely read the remaining chapters of this book and work through the practical assignments.

11–14 Points – Congratulations! You have developed an ability to see and distinguish opportunities. If you continue on this path, you will achieve incredible results in identifying opportunities and use them to achieve greater heights. Remember there are no limits to perfection; continue on the foundation of self-education and improvement and develop your prowess.

15–20 Points – Well done! You are a champion. You have great ability in distinguishing even imperceptible chances and you grasp every opportunity with intensity and tenacity. You will not allow opportunities to pass you by, you take them by the horn, to the next level. Be gracious and share your knowledge and skills with those around you who are yet to reach your level of strength.

Practical Assignments

1. List 10 opportunities you are able to deduce in your life at this moment. Tell us how you plan to use these opportunities. Details your answers with dates, goals and a list of specific plans of action.

2. What is your understanding of this quote from Albert Einstein: "It is impossible to solve a problem at the same level at which it originated, you must rise above the problem, up to the next level"?

3. List signs or characteristics that display a hunger for information. Detail a plan of action to develop your skills and eliminate any lethargy.

4. List and define your strategy to develop the skills you need to identify and seize opportunities.

Chapter 3

THOSE WHO TAKE ADVANTAGE OF OPPORTUNITIES

Chapter 3
THOSE WHO TAKE ADVANTAGE OF OPPORTUNITIES

In the previous chapter we addressed how our internal mind affects our ability to notice emerging opportunities in our path. In this short chapter, we will focus on the categories of people who are prone to seizing opportunities as they come. Studies confirm that opportunities are available to everyone, however these two categories of people have been identified to possess the right attributes to detect opportunities:

1. Those who are eagerly looking for an opportunity, who are thoughtful of their surroundings and deliberate in their actions in their search for opportunities in any situation or circumstance they find themselves in.

2. Those who are prepared for any eventuality by developing their knowledge and skills either through training, formal or informal education or self-study

through the reading of books or researching via the Internet, etc.

In this first category, those who are consciously looking for chance and seeking opportunities operate with the knowledge that "if you do not look, you will not find". These people are in the state of constant expectation, so when opportunities arise they are ready to grasp them. These individuals are conscious of their surroundings and work on the basis that one possibility always leads to another. This mind-set is firmly backed up by the well-known biblical principle: "Ask and it will be given to you; seek and you will find; knock and the door will be opened to you. For everyone who asks receives; the one who seeks finds; and to the one who knocks, the door will be opened," Matthew 7:7–8. Ask, look and knock are all verbs conveying action; in order to get to something, to find or achieve the desired results, it is necessary to take action. When a person chooses to "ask", it is necessary to be able to identify or describe what you are asking for – this may be demonstrated by sight but is not exclusive to it, as it can also be conceived in the mind.

The next point of action will be "knock", as prescribed by the above verse. We must knock on every possible door – by taking all necessary steps in seeking we will discover possibilities in ways and places beyond our comprehension. It is a promise after all. The onus is on us to take all, as prescribed consistently. "Good things comes to those who wait" is one of the biggest deceptions of all time. Better things come to those who seek. By our action and persistence, we will encourage opportunities to come our way. It is necessary to prepare in addition to ask, seek and knock. As we make use of the opportunities in our path new opportunities are generated. Much like our bodies, when we exercise them we generate stronger muscles, and if we fail to exercise them our muscles become weak. A person who has been through physical rehabilitation following a car accident may better understand this analogy.

The second category are those who are prepared and able to recognise opportunities. Preparation helps in identifying opportunities as they cross our path. Preparation is the dominant ability that determines if the opportunity coming our way is seized or ignored. For example, if you are a highly qualified specialist in precious stones, you understand all the intricacies of a precious stone, so when you see a raw stone by the side of the road you will be inclined to pick it up and investigate further. You will have an appreciation which will not be common in an ordinary person who has not prepared and sought the knowledge you have on stones. The preparation which must have been done before an opportunity arises is a catalyst for the ability to convert possibilities into reality. To identify value in places or situations which others fail to notice, you must prepare.

Sam Walton, the founder of Walmart, is an example of a simple man who created a billion-dollar business. What opportunities did he have that propelled him to success? How was he able to use these opportunities to his advantage? Walton was a small town wholesale grocery trader. When his stores were under the pressure of competition and on the verge of closing down, rather than going out of business and accepting defeat, he began to travel around the country. He visited all the major chain stores in his line of business. In his visits and observations, he took note of his likes and dislikes, paying particular attention to what was missing or lacking in the industry. Walton's experiences opened his eyes and gave him an idea in the area of discounted products. This was the niche he took as an opportunity to take his business to the next level. His visits to other stores and his action of identifying what his competitors were doing gave him an advantage, and an opportunity he seized, to understand his market better. In his own words, Walton admitted "I stole, or should I say, borrowed, many ideas from the best at the time…I visited the headquarters of the company and asked to head the meeting as a representative of a small trader from Arkansas. Often I was ignored, but sometimes out of curiosity I was welcomed to the meetings. I asked many questions about the excellent work the companies are doing, and I was given answers to satisfy my interests. I learned so much from there of what I had to implement."

This is an important lesson from the account of Sam Walton. He took several steps, some of which I would even say were brave. The idea of visiting competitors and even asking to join in meetings as a representative of a small trader is simple and yet genius. The courage is to be commended, as in the end his hard work paid dividends, even to this day. To be successful in life you must be bold and have the audacity to execute your ideas until they become reality.

The second purpose of Sam Walton's trip was to find the best employees at all the leading businesses he visited, gathering these talents together to find out what drove them to be the best in what they do. He was relentless in his pursuit for the best employees; wherever he found excellence in an employee, regardless of the sector, he would persuade the employee to work for Walmart. He did this for many years and was able to build his dream team of Walmart talent. By 1968, Walton had opened 34 stores. His idea was summarised at the final stage of formation as follows: "We had a clear concept of retail, core professional management and distribution that could support the company's rapid growth." The key to Walton's success was vision; he focused on his vison and was persistent and intense in his pursuit.

Sam Walton's success was preceded by preparation. The level of his success matched his preparation. He did not wait for opportunities to find him. During a turbulent time in his business, he stood for what he believed in and seized the chance to venture out of his comfort zone by leaving his hometown and business to seek solutions. Could Walton have been afraid during these times? Yes, maybe, maybe not – in any case he did what he had to do and even endured the humiliation of rejection in order to seize the opportunities to develop his business. He did his part to stay afloat in an era of change, he went above and beyond to improve his business and achieve success. As a result, he not only survived, he also became the number one retailer of his time. Sam Walton is a striking example of the category of people who take advantage of opportunities as they appear. With the courage to search for opportunities in the area of his calling, he focused and proactively sought solutions with actions to achieve his goal. Sam Watson demonstrated clearly that without courage, there would be no prosperity.

To take advantage of opportunities, you must be prepared – preparation in the knowledge that opportunity will definitely come and you have to be ready to make use of it. But it is not enough to possess valuable knowledge and experience – in addition to knowledge and experience you most make a move, take steps, take action and knock on doors until you find. Then it is safe to say that the opportunities will not pass you by. In the path of seeking you will discover more of your abilities, generating even more opportunities and success. The phrase "the rich get richer" describes this well. Don't wait for opportunity to come to you, start to take action toward your goal.

Golden Nuggets

1. To discover opportunity, it is your responsibility to search for it.

2. Ask and it will be given to you, seek and you will find, knock and the door will be opened to you. Those who ask, receive; the one who seeks, finds; and to the one who knocks, the door will open. Let this be a reminder to you, and use it as your motivation as you take steps towards your goals.

3. Preparation precedes opportunity. To see value where nobody sees anything of value, you need to be prepared. These popular, great words to live by will be

of benefit to you; the 5Ps are **Prior Preparation Prevents Poor Performance.**

4. Opportunities will be found by those who are know how to recognise opportunity.

Self-Examination Test

Take this test to help you identify how well you are able to determine opportunities in your life:

1. How would you respond to an engagement to speak in front of an audience?
a) Not my thing – 0 points;
b) I don't have any reason to speak in front of an audience – 1 point;
c) It would be challenging, but I will give it a go – 2 points;
d) I relish the opportunity, bring it on – 4 points.

2. How do you deal with conflict?
a) I don't – 0 points;
b) I avoid conflict – 1 point;
c) Take my time, then sum up the courage – 2 points;
d) I can articulate my concerns and express my feelings in a way that is clear, direct and appropriate – 4 points.

3. How do you defend your personal opinion, especially if it differs from the majority's?

a) Majority usually wins, so I don't bother – 0 points;

b) It requires considerable effort, only if it is worth my time – 1 point;

c) I will make my point and hope they understand – 2 points;

d) I will focus on the point without getting defensive – 4 points.

4. Do you systematically strive for your goals, in spite of challenges?

a) No – 0 points;

b) Not necessarily – 1 point;

c) More yes than no – 3 points;

d) Absolutely – 4 points.

5. I usually lose the desire to seek a distant goal, if something is in the way.

a) Yes – 0 points;

b) Usually – 1 point;

c) I try not to let challenges get in my way – 3 points;

d) No! Challenge is all part of the motivation. Bring it on! – 4 points.

Test Results

5 Points or Lower – You do not take advantage of opportunities even when they are served on a silver platter for you. Use this book as an opportunity to develop yourself. Start with the determination to succeed in learning and develop the courageous attitude and character you need to seek and seize opportunities. Take the bold step to seek at least 5 opportunities daily and make a conscious decision to take actions to achieve a goal. It is recommended you continue to read this book thoroughly, answering all the questions at the end of each chapter and completing the practical assignments. These will aid your understanding of areas where you must concentrate your development.

6–10 Points – Your ability to seek and seize is non-existent. To be successful you must change your attitude and outlook on life. Don't be discouraged; you have the ability to change and develop the tools you need to seek and seize opportunities. Make it your life goal to see opportunity in every situation. Identify no less than five opportunities daily. Develop a positive belief system and let it drive your action. Diligently work through the remaining part of this book.

11–14 Points – This is not a bad score! But it could be better. You may be wondering why you are not where you want to be with your goals. In order to convert your ideas and dreams into reality you must intensify your efforts. Develop the courage to seek and seize opportunities and take timely actions. Determination coupled with consistent action will eventually pay off. Be bold, take everything from life as it generously provides.

15–20 Points – Congratulations! You have entered into the category of people who can successfully take advantage of opportunities without any hindrance. Why don't you spread the power and share your skills with those who are not as successful in finding and recognising opportunities in their own lives?

Practical Assignments

1. Life itself is an opportunity. Is this statement true or false? Expand on your answer.

2. What is wrong with waiting patiently for an opportunity?

3. Identify and list ten opportunities in your life. Develop an action plan for each opportunity to become a success. Your action plan must be backed up with dates and priority level.

Chapter 4

HOW TO BEST TAKE ADVANTAGE OF AN OPPORTUNITY

Chapter 4
HOW TO BEST TAKE ADVANTAGE OF AN OPPORTUNITY

In the previous chapter we identified the type of people who best take advantage of opportunities. Two categories of people were identified: those who actively seek opportunities and those who diligently prepare to be able to recognise opportunities. In this chapter, we will forge ahead to learn how to respond to opportunities.

A coach came to training with a bag of candy. At the start of the training he put the candy in the centre of the room and shouted out loud for all to hear, "These candies are luck candies, any candy from this bag will bring you luck once eaten!" Let's pause for a minute – what do you think should happen after this announcement? Do you think everyone will rush to get the luck candy? There were 30 people in the room, and of the 30 only a fraction of the people took the offer. The others sat and laughed at the two or three who stood up to get the luck candy. What is the moral of this story? Before the lessons are explained, answer this question: what would you do if you were in this same scenario? Would you get up and take a candy? Answer this question honestly.

Five minutes later, the bag of candy was cleared and the offer taken off the table. The coach gave a "debriefing". He asked the following questions:

1. Why did you take the candy?

2. Why did you not take the candy?

This is how the fun began! Here are answers from those who took the candies:

- I want to be happy

- I like taking chances, being spontaneous gives me life. I have nothing to lose from taking and eating the luck candy

All other responses border on the individual choice to do something to affect their own happiness.

Interestingly the group of people who decided to go for the "luck candy" were people who were already living a happy life; they were observed to have most things they wanted in life, at least in a material sense.

The majority who did not show any interest in the "luck candy" were asked a similar question, "Why didn't you take the candy?" These were their responses:

- I don't believe in fairy tales

- I don't believe in luck

- I don't want to be deceived

- I don't want to raise my hopes for nothing

- I don't know why I didn't take the candy

On analysis of the answers concerning the luck candy, it is clear the need to be happy and successful plays a key role in the decision to take a chance or not. Their choices inform and affirm their reality. Those who did not take the candy admittedly confirmed they were unsuccessful, poor and unhappy, and yet unwilling to take the offer of the luck candy. Those who really desired the possibilities of what the candy could offer took the steps required for the possibility to realise the benefit of luck.

The fact from this scenario is simple: happiness is a choice, and success is a choice. The path to both happiness and success is presented to all, the choice to take it is yours to take. Those who desire happiness and success take the steps necessary to achieve it, even in uncertainty. The alternative is to do nothing and be sure to achieve nothing. No excuses, just your choice to create your reality.

When faced with any situation, good or bad, it can be resolved in the knowledge that the situation will also present opportunities – how you search them out and what you do with them is up to you. The key to identifying opportunities in a situation is to:

• See excuses as not an option; doing nothing is not an option. Act!

• Be grateful for the chance

These are the two responses to opportunities that will prevent a miss or a loss. Let's now look at a short story about a remarkable man.

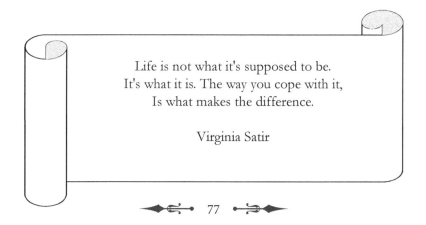

Life is not what it's supposed to be.
It's what it is. The way you cope with it,
Is what makes the difference.

Virginia Satir

The Story of the Blind Pilot

Miles Hilton-Barber was born on December 20, 1948 in Harare, Zimbabwe. As a teenager, he decided to follow in his father's footsteps to become a pilot. Miles was accepted into flight school, but did not pass the medical examination because of his sight. Three years later he was given the devastating news that he has a genetic predisposition which would render him completely blind. As predicted, by the age of 30 Miles had gone completely blind.

As his sight was deteriorating, he moved to England and worked at the Royal National Institute for the Blind. In an account of his past, Miles Hilton-Barber says, "I was afraid to even walk 400 meters to the nearest supermarket for a loaf of bread." The drastic change which led to a turning point in his life was his younger brother, Jeff. It so happened that Jeff was also blind, but he noticed that it did not stop him from achieving his goals. Jeff planned to go on a single voyage in his yacht from Africa to Australia, and he did. This attitude of determination and self-belief changed his older brother's attitude to blindness and inspired him to realise his own dream.

In his fifties Miles Hilton-Barber began to participate in sports marathons, rock climbing and flights on small aircrafts. In 1998 he took part in the London Marathon, and in 1999 overcame one of the toughest marathons across the Sahara Desert. In 2000, he climbed to the top of Mount Kilimanjaro. The same year he attempted to conquer the distance from the coast of Antarctica to the South Pole on a sleigh. In 2001, he ran a marathon in China, and in 2002, in Siberia. In the same year he was part of a team of three people with disabilities, whose purpose was to travel around the world with more than 80 types of transport. In 2003 he became the first blind pilot who flew over the English Channel on a passenger plane.

This adventurer has many more achievements and accolades. Not to mention, among other things, Hilton-Barber is also a motivational speaker. Using his personal example to inspire many people around the world, he encourages others to live their dreams and not allow circumstances to hold them back. What have you learnt from the story of Miles Hilton-Barber and his younger brother Jeff? What would be your considerations in the same circumstances? How do you handle adversity? These are questions we must always ponder, knowing there are opportunities in every situation.

We often have a habit of exaggerating our problems, using challenges as excuses. If you can think something negative, you can also think the same situation positive. The difference is where we choose to place our mental allegiance. We must be stronger than our strongest excuse. Miles changed his thinking in order to have new and better experiences. His condition of blindness did not change but his experience and quality of life changed. When he changed his thinking and removed his mental limits his dreams became his reality and he began to inspire others. Excuses are just an unwillingness to act or take positive action, not objective reasons for failure. "Doing nothing is doing something", so in that case why not actually choose to do something? What you really want to do. Hilton argues that "the only obstacle to success is 5 cm between our ears". If we allow this 5 cm, it will deprive us of the most precious experiences in life.

Do You Live a Life of Excuses?

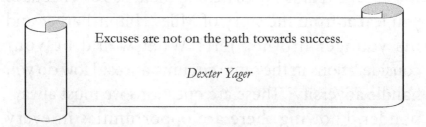

Excuses are not on the path towards success.

Dexter Yager

Have you ever come across people with one excuse or another? You included, right? I have no money, I have no time, I don't know. These are the "naysayers" who spend all their lives concentrating on problems, feeling sorry for themselves. Remember in the story of Ivan Spade, he has a good job and a reasonable salary, he could have started a business if he wanted to. Tamara the housewife has lots of time and could use her time as she chooses. Victor Smead just graduated from university, the world is his oyster. Although their situations are different, they are all equally entitled to take opportunities that life has to offer. Many people look at successful people with the delusion that they were born successful. In reality every success has a start which has no resemblance to the outcome. What are your buts? The achievements you see today started off looking very different, tiresome and unattractive, but someone was determined to focus and intensify their efforts until the goal was achieved.

Victor Smead started teaching in schools and supplementing his income with private tutoring. He did this for many years until he was able to find a better position. He exceeded the role requirement, giving 100% at work, and this led to promotions and subsequent prominence in the company.

a mother of five and a farmer, gets
morning to milk cows ready f
dawn. James, a young graduate, \
time. Throughout his studies at
juggle work in order to stay in sc

happ

variety; just as our lives are different so are the opportunities available to us.

Justifying your situation with all manner of excuses will not work in your favour. Justification is an attempt to reduce your guilt and to diminish your responsibility to attain success. No matter who it is, everybody goes through difficult circumstances in life; there is no life exempt from the challenges of life. The key is not to allow the challenges of life to overwhelm you. What separates the winners from the losers is the choices they make and these choices are a product of how the situation is interpreted. "The death of success begins with a series of symptoms called excuses," says Brendon Burchard, an American author on motivation, high performance and online marketing. He is the number one *New York Times* bestselling author of *The Millionaire Messenger*. You must consciously master your world and character, be accountable for the choices you make. Excuses are immersed in the depth of human worthlessness, rendering humans powerless. If a person begins to think and act like a victim of circumstance, it is very difficult to remain master of their life. Success is only found in those who are masters of their lives.

People who believe they control their lives are ier than those who believe that their lives are controlled by someone else. Lack of control will develop into frustration and unhappiness, which will result in keeping success at bay. People who blame external factors for the consequences of their actions are not wise; they in the end lose out on the opportunities to develop from the lessons of the action. Playing the blame game is one of the most destructive human behaviours, it is better curtailed sooner rather than later.

Those who are in control of their lives are not influenced by others – they use others' opinions as a stepping stone and not a stumbling block. Successful people are their own cheerleaders, others cheering them on or not will not impact their goals. The outcome of your work, good or bad, is fully your responsibility, you must have self-belief and be rational in your approach. When others control your life, you surrender your rights and dreams, you are in effect a puppet in someone else's show.

If you are prone to thinking others are guilty of your failures, you will gradually become angry at the people and the world around you, and as a result, get into circumstances that contribute to your anger. You are what you think; what you are as you read this book is as a result of your thought. Once you diminish your responsibility for your life, you lost the ability to change and affect your life for the better. Blaming others is admitting failure, and shows that you lack vision. "Where there is no vision, the people perish," Proverb 29:18. Death does not just occur when blood stops pumping into the heart. When you concede to the belief system that others are to be blamed for your situation, that is an indication of lack of vision and therefore as it says in the Proverb, the outcome is to perish.

Successful people start with the self-belief that they can achieve their goals and that the power to affect their lives is in their hands. They find a way to do, in any circumstances even against all odds, as with the story of Hilton-Barber and Jeff. Determination is essential – nobody and nothing can stop a person in control from fulfilling their plan. Their self-belief and self-talk is positive and empowering: "I am responsible for my life and able to take the necessary actions to affect my life." SUCCESSFUL PEOPLE TAKE RESPONSIBILITY FOR THEIR LIVES. They understand that they are responsible for their own failures, so they are able to change their cause and learn from mistakes. Such people do not make excuses – they seek, see and seize opportunities to change their lives according to their earnest goals.

A Life of Excuses Leads to Lost Opportunities

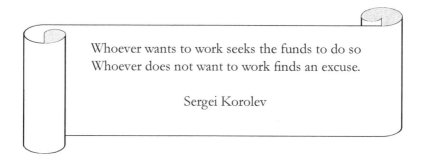

Whoever wants to work seeks the funds to do so
Whoever does not want to work finds an excuse.

Sergei Korolev

How does justifying failure and excuses lead to lost opportunities? If a person blames circumstances and others except himself, he gives permission to the situation and concedes to defeat. Many fall into this trap when an opportunity is lost, but the worst thing about this way of thinking is that the person also fails to identify the lessons and learn from them. The excuse becomes a double-edged sword when the lessons are not learnt. In the deception of excuses, it is impossible to find the need to change; blame puts the responsibility of change on the shoulders of others. It is a defeatist mentality, not accepting responsibility for the fact that you are one hundred percent responsible for your life. Responsibility for your own life leads to control over it, and control promotes positive change in you and ultimately success.

If you are in the category of people who blame others, this is an opportunity to accept the power and acknowledge where you have faltered. Start by acknowledging that you are ultimately responsible for your choices – your parents, the government, your employer, your boss and any other person in your life is NOT to blame and is not responsible for what happens in your life. Let me put it plainly, the state of the economy does not matter – whether you live in a developed country or not, everything that happens in your life depends entirely on what is in your head, the thoughts that prevail in your mind. When you accept and acknowledge this fact, the possibilities for success are endless and you start to see new occurrences that will develop into opportunities to achieve your goals. Do not allow excuses and blame to cut you off from new opportunities.

The saddest consequences of excuses are the negative footprints they leave. The trap is in the repetition of the excuses; this is absorbed into our subconscious mind and deepens into a belief system and becomes reality. It is a proven fact that those who get opportunities seek to find them.

Do not waste your life on useless and dangerous mind-numbing excuses and the blame culture. In order to cultivate the right responses to opportunities, you must destroy the captivity of excuses and blame. A destructive consequence of blame and excuses is that it undermines your confidence in your ability to effect change.

A Life of Gratitude Opens Doors to New Opportunities

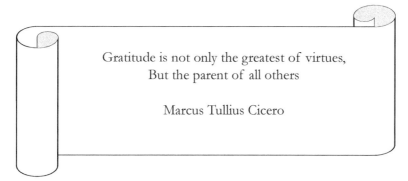

Gratitude is not only the greatest of virtues,
But the parent of all others

Marcus Tullius Cicero

According to Ushakov's *Russian Dictionary*, "gratitude" means a sense of appreciation for good, devotion or service. Please note the words "good" and "service". It is important to do good by serving others. In doing good to others and in service to others you plant a seed, which multiplies and produces possibilities.

Gratitude opens doors to the heart of others or to possibilities, it yields a positive outcome. Studies by a group of scientists at the University of Florida in Tallahassee (USA), under the supervision of Professor Nathaniel Lambert, found that the degree of satisfaction in the relationships of people depend on the verbal ability to express gratitude. The finding shows that **the more often words of gratitude are communicated in**

a relationship, the stronger the couple. A good relationship is perhaps the most important requirement; this is pivotal in taking advantage of opportunities. Think about it: when you have built a good relationship with others, there is the willingness to share information, ideas and opportunities.

Acknowledgements are important not only for the recipient but also the giver. The act of gratitude produces a win-win outcome in any situation. Gratitude strengthens relationships, it increases our responsibility for others. It also contributes to the satisfaction of all parties involved as observed in the study by Professor Lambert: "When you express gratitude, it forces your focus on the good others have done for you."

Studies by Japanese and American psychologists led by Keiko Otake at the University of Kwansei Gakuin and Kobe College Japan, show that those who are used to expressing gratitude in everyday life are highly optimistic, have a sense of harmony and are physically healthier. Those who show gratitude are happier and prone to positive thinking. Gratitude unites the world, and it is particularly relevant in today's global community and the advent of technology, which has opened the world to communicate beyond borders. Gratitude is a powerful tool, with potential that outweighs the act. A GRATEFUL HEART IS A HAPPY

LIFE. Take this as your cue to create a positive attitude and feel the happiness in yourself, and see the changes it creates in your life.

Therapist Margarita Zhamkochyan confirms the impact of gratitude: "Gratitude focuses attention on the positive events in life and as a result, prevents the mind from frustration. It encourages us to experience more positive emotions, drawing attention to good fortune and opening doors to achieve our goals." As a direct result of this way of thinking, we generally begin to experience more positivity in life.

Unfortunately, only a small percentage of people have the ability to show gratitude; most people are too self-absorbed to make gratitude a way of life. The value derived from a grateful heart surpasses the simplicity of the act. When we cultivate thanking God and humans, we experience a fulfilment in our relationships and life in general. One of the world's most renowned experts on leadership, Robin Sharma, a Canadian writer and leadership speaker, observed in his studies that the main reason why talented people leave companies is not low pay but that they do not feel the gratitude of the employer. His advice to management is to build a team in which gratitude is the foundation and where hard work, innovative thinking and an innovative approach are encouraged and rewarded.

Showing gratitude should be a lifestyle as a positive attitude will yield a positive life. At worst, the same amount of work is needed to be miserable as it is to be positive. If you remember the law of sowing and reaping, you will understand that you cannot be negative and expect to live a positive life. What you sow is what you reap, to which everything in the universe is subjected. Randy Gage, an American author and motivational speaker who writes self-help books and lectures on the subjects of success and prosperity, explains the seven laws of prosperity. These laws have been proved invaluable over the years and I will suggest you develop and live by these laws in order to manifest true prosperity. It will also aid you in your response and ability to create opportunities for others.

Here are the Seven Laws of Prosperity in a nutshell:

1. Law of Nothingness

If you need a new pair of shoes, discard the old ones. If you need new clothes, clear out your closet. Of your own accord, separate yourself from your old stereotypes.

2. Law of Circulation

Be willing to let go of something that you own to get something you want.

3. **Law of Imagination**

You must be able to see your life as you want it to be in your imagination; you have to see your prosperity in your imagination. Write down your ideal day, have it handy and read it to yourself as often as you can, at least once daily.

4. **Law of Creativity**

A person can achieve prosperity through the energy of his thinking, intuition and imagination.

5. **Law of Retribution and Receiving**

If you give something away, it comes back ten-fold. When you receive something good, it is very important to share it with others. If you have a talent and do not use it, you insult yourself and your maker. To treat your abilities with due reverence, you should rejoice in your gifts and share them with others. If you do this, you attract more wealth into your life.

6. **Law of Tithing**

This is one of the key principles to increasing wealth, earnestly giving 10% of all you have as it increases. This can be given in any form, just make sure it leaves your hand to benefit others.

7. Act of Atonement

If you cannot forgive, you cannot take your wealth. If your soul is filled with hate, love cannot find its place. You must get rid of the negative feelings that do not give you peace. Light and dark do not dwell together.

So we have learnt how gratitude is capable of attracting new opportunities in our lives. Let's take a look at what we should be thankful for.

As you keep your mind and heart focused in the right direction, approaching each day with faith and gratitude, I believe you will be empowered to live life to the fullest and enjoy the abundant life He has promised you!

Victoria Osteen

Five Things to be Grateful For

It is important to understand where and for what we should be grateful. After all, only someone who is grateful is worthy of the blessings of gratitude.

1. **Accept your uniqueness as a privilege.** Understand and be grateful for your uniqueness, like each snowflake that falls to the ground. The individuality of each person consists of a uniqueness and originality from the creator, this sense was expressed by Nikolai Gogol, a Russian dramatist, novelist and short story writer of Ukrainian ethnicity in one of his classic works. Every person on this planet, including you, is unique and deserves to live in abundance, joy, health and all intended for him by his creator. All you need to do is to receive what already belongs to you. The man who has learned to accept himself is able to take all the opportunities that are available in his path.

2. **Thank God for your parents and thank them directly.** Parents must be given gratitude and respect by their children, according to the Great Russian Empress Catherine II. The role of parents is unique in the life of a child. Good or bad they are our route to this world. And through them we have other unique connections, our character, traits, features and even identity through genetics. Ultimately as we reach the age of accountability, our life is in our hands. Opportunities that arise in our lives depend on how we learn to express our appreciation and gratitude for our parents and our nearest and dearest. It is necessary to learn how important the expression of respect and care is for our parents and family.

3. **All of our life experience help us to become who we are now.** We are a product of all the compiled worries we experience in life. This could be our direct or indirect experiences from the lives of others, close friends or relatives, even what we learn from afar (social media and the news). We must cultivate the habit of thanking life for what it has done for us. This may seem silly to you but it is necessary as a process to get the best out of life. Through trial and error, we become who we are: errors if correctly perceived, make people stronger by strengthening their character. Life is where we live. If we do not appreciate and show gratitude for where we are living our lives, we will miss the opportunities it brings because we fail to embrace this key principle. Don't abdicate responsibility for your life, and do not play the blame game. Don't dwell on your mistakes, accept responsibility when you falter, learn the lessons and move on. You are human and prone to make mistakes. The more mistakes you make and learn from, the more successful you will become in life. Success rests on mistakes: when you encounter problems or make mistakes, in trying to overcome them you will gain valuable lessons. You will learn what works and what does not work. Mistakes are the route to success; don't be afraid to make mistakes. "An expert is a person who has made all possible mistakes in a very narrow specialty," – Niels Bohr, a Danish physicist and public figure, one of the founders of modern physics.

"Comfort zones almost immediately become confinement zones," – Brian Bird. Embrace mistakes as your propeller to success.

The key to converting failure to success is to learn how to draw lessons from your mistakes. If the lessons are not learned it is likely you will make the same mistakes again. As you learn from each mistake, you move closer to success. New mistakes lead to success, recurring mistakes lead to frustration. Once lessons are leaned from mistakes, you must also learn how to implement the lessons to achieve greater heights and gain access to new opportunities.

Be thankful and take nothing for granted. We often take peace for granted in the country in which we live. The food on our table, the house we live in, good health, ability to speak, walk and the use of our hands, eyes and ears. These are simple things we must not forget to appreciate. Make the most of what you have now and you will not suffer regret when it is no more. According to Daniel Defoe, English writer and publicist, all our complaints about what we lack stem from a lack of gratitude for what we do have. Let us learn to appreciate what we already possess and only then will we open the door of abundance. Learn to recognise value in everything, there are values in everything and often not obvious at first glance. Getting up in the morning should be enough to be thankful; the adage, "where there is life there is hope", rings true when you have an attitude of gratitude for the simplest things in life.

4. **Always remember the people who have helped you along the way.** The law of gratitude is the application of the law of "cause and effect". The universal law of cause and effect states that for every effect there is a definite cause, and likewise for every cause there is a definite effect. Your thoughts, behaviours and actions create specific effects that manifest and create your life as you know it. Much like the principle of what you sow, you reap, when we show gratitude in response to the assistance of other people we provoke the manifestation of gratitude to us; our efforts and good deeds will not be in vain. However, if we ignore the law of gratitude in our lives, we force people and the universe itself to ignore us. The whole world will remain deaf and unresponsive to our pleas for help when we need it.

It is important to be thankful for the strangers that offer to help, any kind word or smile given. According to Robert Emmons, a social psychologist, professor of psychology at UC Davis and researcher of the phenomenon of gratitude, "The more we thank others, the more they appreciate us, the warmer towards us they get, and we generate new reasons to be grateful". The consequence of this, as explained by the scientist, is a tangible improvement of the quality of our lives.

To respond well to opportunities, it is important to **cultivate regular thankfulness.** The idea is to enter into a state of gratitude and stay in it forever. The principle is to be thankful for what you have now, without ceasing to strive to new heights. The reason why ordinary people take so long to achieve their goals is that we focus on what we do not have, we complain about what is out of our reach, neglecting opportunities right in front of us. We send the wrong messages out to the universe, the messages of lack: "I do not have it", "I cannot get it" – and as a result, give more power to what we say being our reality. To break out of this, repeat what you want and the positivity you envision instead of speaking about the lack you fear. Luke 19:26 says: "I tell you that to everyone who has, more will be given, but as for the one who has nothing, even what they have will be taken away." Professing what you do not have or lack will result in having nothing. It almost becomes a self-fulfilling prophecy.

"For a smart person gratitude is not a painful feeling," said the English writer Edward E. Bulwer-Lytton. When you learn to be grateful for all the opportunities you already have you will be pleasantly surprised with how your life will be improved, not only for your own good, but for the benefit of others too. A grateful heart will open up spectacular new opportunities; take advantage of the power of gratitude, embrace this simple act and enjoy the harvest of fulfilment. Always remember and regularly use this simple statement of "Thank you".

Golden Nuggets

1. Take responsibility, don't play the blame game or make excuses

2. Be grateful to God in every situation. Your current situation is not your final destination.

3. There are opportunities in your current situation, be thankful and your gratitude will unlock new opportunities.

4. If you truly have a need, do everything you can to attain it; giving up is not an option, you must grab every opportunity like your life depends on it.

5. Excuses are just an unwillingness to take corrective action. Doing nothing is doing something to guarantee failure.

6. You are what you think. If you think like a victim of circumstance, then it is very difficult for you to be master of your life to discover new opportunities.

7. People who believe that they control their lives are happier and have greater opportunities than those who believe that their lives are controlled by others.

8. Excuses and blame leads to lost opportunities.

9. Whoever wants success looks for opportunities, those who will not look find excuses.

10. Gratitude propels new opportunities.

11. Gratitude helps to focus on the positive experiences of life. It also dispels frustration. It encourages us to experience positive emotions, focusing our attention on our fortunes.

12. Whoever is grateful for what he receives, is worthy of more benefits.

13. To find new opportunities, be thankful for what you have now and strive for new heights.

This test will give you some insight on how you distinguish opportunities in your life:

Self-Examination Test

1. Which of the following best describes you?

a) Other people don't understand what I am going through – 0 points;

b) I am trying my best but things are not easy – 2 points;

c) Some things happen that I cannot control, but I don't let it get to me. – 3 points;

d) My life, my choices – 4 points.

2. How often do you use this phrase? "I was busy"

a) Always – 0 points;

b) Quite often – 1 point;

c) Rarely – 3 points;

d) Always never – 4 points.

3. How often do you show appreciation to others by saying "thank you"?

a) Always never – 0 points;

b) Rarely – 1 point;

c) Frequently – 3 points;

d) Always – 4 points.

4. How would you assess the level of your gratitude to life?

a) What should I be thankful for? – 0 points;

b) I admit, I am a very ungrateful person. – 2 points;

c) I strive to be grateful – 3 points;

d) I am grateful to every person and for every little thing – 4 points.

Test Results

Up to 4 Points – Unfortunately, you fail to see opportunities in your path. You miss opportunities because the level of excuses in your life is overwhelming. If you continue in this way you are likely to diminish the possibility of any opportunity opening up to you. To develop the skills to seek and seize opportunities you must start with gratitude from this very moment. There is so much to be grateful for, the gift of life and hope. You should not have to think deeply before you find a reason to be grateful. This book will also teach you how to align yourself to be grateful and learn to seize opportunities in life. Continue to read this book thoroughly and complete the practical assignments in each chapter.

5–8 Points – You are aware of opportunities in your life but often have the wrong attitude so you miss them. The likelihood is that you are missing these chances because of your lack of gratitude and level of excuses. Once you start to change your mind-set and develop an appreciation for life and for people you will in turn find that things start to change for you for the better. Continue diligently to read and complete the remaining part of this book. Do not be discouraged, there is hope, if you are willing to do what it takes you will surely reap the benefits.

9–12 Points – You do not often make excuses and you do see a need to be grateful. However, you need to develop the attitude of gratitude to a greater height. Increase your efforts to identify the good things in life and use your discoveries as the stepping stones to open the doors of opportunity and attain your dream. Continue to read this book and your change will come as you constantly take the steps necessary to achieve your goal.

13–16 Points – Congratulations! You have the ability to seek and seize opportunities. This is your domain and you have mastered it. You take accountability for your life and your goals, you are relentless in your pursuit and give your very best in showing appreciation to people and in life generally. As you may already know, there are many more great opportunities that await you. Start sharing your know-how with others, lifting others up to be able to enjoy all life has to offer.

Practical Assignments

1. The candy scenario – What would you do if you were in this scenario? What is your opinion of it? From your point of view, is this scenario an opportunity or a game without benefit? Let's assume you don't like candy – given the luck element of the candies what would you do? What are your conclusions based on this scenario? What impact does this scenario have on your life, what lessons have you learned from it?

2. Review the level of your habit to make excuses. What steps will you take to reduce the level of excuses you make?

3. Write a list of what you are grateful for in your life, past and present – this can be anything. Write down everything that comes to mind, and every day, come back to this list, reading it over, adding to the list as you remember new reasons to be grateful.

4. Develop the habit of giving thanks for all the good in your life and the world in general. Make it your habit each night before you go to bed – list all the good things that happened throughout the day and thank God. Let you heart be glad in everything, no matter how small or simple it may seem to you. These actions will generate more of the beauty you are grateful for and create opportunities to receive in abundance.

Chapter 5

LIFE
IS AN OPPORTUNITY
TO SERVE

Chapter 5
LIFE IS AN OPPORTUNITY TO SERVE

It is bad if no one cares about you.
But it is even worse if you care for no one.

Stanislaw Jerzy Lec

As a teenager, Thomas Edison rescued a three-year-old child. Staring at the tracks right in front of a locomotive train, he bravely took the chance to save the child's life. The child he saved was the youngest son of the station master, who in gratitude taught Edison telegraph code used on the railways at the time. As a result of this event, aged 16, Thomas Alva Edison was given his first prestigious and well-paid job as the station telegraph operator in Port Huron. In those days, telegraph was the most common means of communication; with his experience on the job he became skilled in decoding and transmitting messages, further developing as an electrician and as a repairman.

The event which opened the doors of opportunity for Edison's career was a good deed in relation to saving a child in danger, but it took courage. One may say it is a coincidence as he was just passing, but his responsiveness served him well. Who knows the direction his life would have taken if he had neglected to pay attention to what was happening around him; after all he was merely a child himself, only 16 at the time. We may never know to whom we need to extend a helping hand or foresee any benefit in a deed. The lesson here is to help others and do our best to effect positive change. As we serve others, then we truly begin to manifest the benefits of "time and chances" in our reality.

The sooner you realise that if a person only lives for him or herself with the resultant problems, illness, adversity, fear and anxiety that causes, the sooner you would accept life as an opportunity. In order be fulfilled in life, you need to serve: our purpose is always linked to services. Our life on earth is a gift, given to us for a short time as an opportunity to serve God and humanity. It is necessary to invest in yourself as well as others to be fulfilled in your life. Those who live only to satisfy their own needs are living for themselves and will eventually become casualties of their existence. Sooner or later, humanity will forget them and they will come and go, never to be remembered. Such a person becomes a slave to his desires, a "Me, Myself and I" person, a closed vessel from which it is impossible to be replenished. We are on earth to serve God by serving people. All that God has given each of us has only one purpose: to serve God by loving and serving others. Your talent, time and treasures are given to you for a purpose, and that purpose can only be served by service to the world through people. In so doing, you serve and honour God. If you do anything else with your talent and treasures other than honour God and serve humanity, you are simply wasting your time in self-denial of the opportunities in life. Take the example of having knowledge in an area and having the ability to teach. What is the point of this knowledge and ability if you don't engage yourself with others to impart your knowledge? Think about it – having financial wealth in the absence of people to spend it with is meaningless. You must have heard and seen people who are wealthy yet unfulfilled and unhappy, even to the extreme of committing suicide. Whatever we possess, either tangible or intangible, it is for us to be a blessing, an answer to serve God and humanity.

LIFE is a service. All great men have achieved success understanding this law. They understand the essence of their greatness from the onset of any goal, and they are able to focus knowing their money, time and opportunities were not their property. They were merely stewards entrusted with these treasures by God. We are not the giver of all that we have in life – the Master gave these treasures to fulfil His purpose through us. Even our own lives do not belong to us; everything on earth belongs to God. He puts us on earth to take charge and manage these things for a period of time. Your life as a creation of God should be devoted to the creator's goal and purpose for His kingdom. Since you have a creator, you must understand your creator, He is your source and He has provided all you need to function on this earth in abundance. We must seek and seize these in the opportunity called life. Stop the self-pity and self-importance – it is not your life, but God's, so for that reason you need to do His will. The proof of our love for God our creator is to serve His PEOPLE.

How to Recognise Opportunities to Serve

Get used to giving more than you receive. Your life on earth is moment in eternity, we are just a small spark in the orbit of the universe. Since we cannot take anything with us when we leave this earth, we must appreciate and always remember the true meaning of our existence – to serve others. As you wake up each morning, repeat these words: "I'll do well today. I will serve others, I'll take care of others, and I will be kind to others." These are the principles of a successful life. If you relentlessly pursue these goals, to help others and be less concerned about your own self-interest, you will be rewarded with a fulfilled life.

Make it part of your lifestyle to be useful to someone else, using your knowledge, experience and skills to make a difference in other people's lives. Nothing brings more inner satisfaction than being able to utilise your skills for the benefit of others. These simple actions will in turn create a value chain of success. Start by dedicating just a few hours from the 168 hours of the week. Selfless service creates a chain of value; this could be as simple as devoting your time to work in a nursing home, with orphans, or helping a neighbour or a stranger. Teach someone to read or offer to hold a public lecture on the topic that you know so that others can benefit from your knowledge and skills. Leave behind a positive footprint, a lasting legacy. To get what you want from the abundance of life's opportunities, you must be prepared to give what you have, give your knowledge, your skills, devote your time to a good cause and share your treasures. We get what we give – if you offer a smile, a compliment, some attention to a friend or a stranger, you will receive back in tenfold.

- **Share your knowledge and skills with others.** It should also be noted that you learn more by teaching others.

- **Be selfless in your deeds, without expecting anything in return; assist someone who needs your help.** By giving, you grow spiritually, as well as sowing a positive seed which will grow to fruition. As illustrated by the law of sowing and reaping, you reap what you sow; start sowing as it will help you also to create a value chain.

- **Challenge yourself to do better**. Your only competition is you, so do your best always. You will feel better about your efforts and develop inner peace in the knowledge you are giving your very best.

- **The most effective way to wealth and prosperity is to meet needs.** Whether they are material, physical, emotional or spiritual needs, use your talents, skills and ability to benefit others. Share your good fortune, with joy and gratitude. At the very least, ensure one tenth of your income leaves your hands: this could be through donations to charity and giving to or supporting a cause; the key is to make sure one tenth of your income goes out to benefit others. When you help others, you also help yourself to be a better person; what you give will come back to you in multiple folds.

What is the Purpose of a Business?

Opportunities, greatness, success and wealth come to be possible for those who understand that life is not just about the self. Multinational companies such as Coca Cola, Procter and Gamble, McDonald's and Unilever are well known and continue to be successful in the marketplace because their products meet the needs of the masses. Think about this: if the company that produces Coca Cola made it available only to their immediate family members, the world would not have known about the drink we all enjoy so much and it would not have been a success story for over 100 years. Look around you and think about some of the innovations in technology that you enjoy; they were all created and developed to meet needs, and for the masses to benefit from. These companies and others like them have become famous worldwide because they use the principle of service, which is the principle of love for people. They strive to serve the greatest number of people, and this makes them popular and successful. This is the principle of life. The more you serve others, the more God exalts you.

Among the seven great lessons from the success of Henry Ford are two very specific recommendations of service to others:

- **Service to others.** "Service to others is the rent you pay for your room here on Earth," said Muhammad Ali, American professional boxer and activist. He is widely regarded as one of the most significant and celebrated sports figures of the 20th century. Business, dedicated to services, has no need to worry about profit – profit is guaranteed. The secret of success lies in serving others. All successful people serve – the greater the substance of the services, the greater the success. Wealth is created for service and can only be generated through service. "Wealth, exactly like happiness, cannot be achieved by direct search. It comes as a by-product of providing useful services," said Henry Ford.

- **Solve a problem, be a solution.** Most people spend a lot of time and energy going around problems searching for solution. You can be an answer to someone's problem – your knowledge, skills and ability could be the answer. You are a solution, so avail yourself to solve problems. The reward for solving the problems of others is success. You may not solve every problem of humanity, but you have in you the ability to solve problems. The magnitude of your success is in correlation to the problem you solve or the benefit of your solution. Do not waste your time worrying around problems, solve them.

Konosuke Matsushita was a Japanese industrialist who founded Panasonic, the largest Japanese consumer electronics company. Many Japanese regard him as the "god of management" for his ability to combine the pursuit of profit with a humanistic attitude toward employees. Matsushita's business mission was to serve people by developing their skills and talents, reducing poverty and improving the living standards of society.

As you profit monetarily, remember money is just a tool. Make service to others the key objective and the mission for a success life. This is the noblest investment of time. Remember, when all is said and done, the quality of your life is determined by the quality of your contribution to the lives of others. Leave a rich legacy to those who surround you and the world at large.

What Happens When We Refuse to Serve

Selfish people focus only on themselves and complain about life. They are constantly disappointed and frustrated with one thing or the other. There is always something missing, and they always say things are out of their control. The problem with these people is that they are blind to the principle of a successful life. By focusing on themselves they violate this principle, and therefore get caught up in problems because of where they focus their attention. Self-pity, anger, rage and envy become constant companions of those who violate the principle of serving people and being a solution.

People who constantly complain about their lives do not understand that their life is a gift; it is not given to them in order to satisfy their whims. A self-centred life is a meaningless life; even if someone has everything they wanted in life success will still elude them. An empty life is a life devoid of serving and meeting the needs of other people.

Thomas Edison, the genius of invention, suffered as a result of his greed at the beginning of the last century when competition arose in the film industry. Although he made gains increasingly in the technical side, competition overtook him in the arts. Yet even in challenging times, his personal fortune continued to increase with more than a thousand patents. In 1923, *The New York Times* published the revenue from Edison's ventures to be in excess of $15 billion, though almost all his profits were reinvested in the business. He was indifferent to luxury, living a simple life even though he could afford expensive things as he was a modest man., relentless in his pursuit to serve people with his discoveries. The inventor businessman had no restraint; his efforts were to create solutions in every sector without boundaries.

He was particularly fascinated, like many inventors of his time, with the advent of cinema, and he quickly created and patented one of the first cameras, a peep show. At that time the film industry worked together with film distribution. Audiences would insert a nickel into an individual glass unit to watch a movie. This gave birth to the name of the first cinema in the United States, Nickelodeon. As a result of his strong influence in the film industry, for the first fifteen years of the last century all American films were produced and laminated by Edison. A surprising result of this monopoly ended with the creation of Hollywood.

US patent law changed disgruntled directors and producers and one after the other they left the East Coast for the West, choosing California in defiance of Washington's rules; besides, the sunshine state was more conducive to the movie industry. While Edison fought against pirates in 1915, the court ruled against him for monopolising the industry, so he was forced to retreat. By the time work started on the development of the suburbs of Los Angeles, Hollywood had become a powerhouse of the movie industry. This was the only defeat of a man who went after everything in life that he wanted.

We can learn not only from the rise but also from the decline of great people. Edison refused to cooperate with others for the common good and creation. He was interested in his own interests. But, by neglecting others, the great inventor lost opportunities that could have opened new doors for the entire community. The film industry found new ways and opportunities for development, free from the grasp of monopoly by Edison. The stream of life never stops; if you try to stand in its way, it will sweep you away. This was not in fact a defeat at all, as Edison paved the way for others and to many it was an opportunity for others to enter the film industry.

Consequently, the higher purpose of our business and of any business is to fulfil the needs of others, solve problems and enrich the world around us. By meeting the needs of others, we also satisfy our own needs and build for the future. When we refuse to serve people not only will they suffer, but so do we. We deprive ourselves of new opportunities, and the fortune of a better life. We are all connected, and if we do not add value to our time, we have wasted time. Your life is improved only when you make the lives of others better.

God will not ask what kind of car you drive, but how many people you drove with it. The size of your house will be irrelevant, the number of people you accommodated will. The content of the designers in your wardrobe will have no bearing on the number of people you provided with clothing.

Examine the following golden truths as a summary of the lessons from this chapter:

Golden Nuggets

1. A person living only for himself will have a life of misery.

2. Life is a gift of service to others.

3. The only evidence of our love for God is in serving people.

4. Cultivate the habit of giving, even in your wants.

5. Educate yourself, broaden your knowledge and share with others as you learn.

6. Assist someone without expecting a reward in return.

7. Always try your best to help others.

8. The most effective way to wealth is to provide for others. Meet the need of the masses, be the solution to the problem of the masses.

9. Nothing is impossible: greatness, success and wealth are all within reach of those who understand the principle of servicing others.

10. If you do not improve someone's life, you are wasting your time and theirs.

11. Your life is improved only when you make other people's lives better.

The following test will give you an insight into your attitude to service. Take note of your scores to aid your development.

Self-Examination Test

1. Are you often told that you think about others more than yourself?
a) No – 0 points;
b) Rarely – 1 point;
c) Usually – 3 points;
d) Always – 4 points.

2. If anyone is in trouble, do you always try to offer your assistance?
a) No – 0 points;
b) Sometimes – 1 point;
c) Usually – 3 points;
d) Always – 4 points.

3. I am always looking for ways to help others.
a) No – 0 points;
b) Sometimes – 1 point;
c) Usually – 3 points;
d) Always – 4 points.

4. My priority is to look after my interest.
a) Always – 0 points;
b) Mostly – 1 point;
c) Rarely – 3 points;
d) Never – 4 points.

5. Do you believe that the most valuable thing in life is to dedicate your life to other people?
a) No – 0 points;
b) Not really – 1 point;
c) In some cases – 3 points;
d) Yes – 4 points.

Test Results

Up to 5 Points – Your life is devoted to you, yourself and you. You pay zero to very little attention to others where it matters. You are depriving yourself of the opportunities that could enrich your life. You must change your attitude to get the best out of your life. Your opportunities are linked to others; for this reason you must cultivate the right attitude with others.

6–10 Points – You have not developed the desire to serve others. You don't see much value in this and for this reason you are missing opportunities, which will improve your life and help you in fulfilling your destiny. It is vital you change your view on life and learn to love and serve people. Start with those around you. By virtue of reading this book you are obviously keen to change your life, so continue to read and complete all practical assignments.

11–14 Points – You are doing well, but you can do better! You seek to serve the people around you, you need to turn that into a habit and in turn create a value chain to help you meet your needs too. It is obvious you have a kind heart and you are willing to help others; be persistent in service to others as new opportunities await you.

15–20 Points – Congratulations! You see the value in devoting yourself to serving others. You are already familiar with the benefit of service to others. Your selfless sacrifice will not go unrewarded. Continue to seize opportunities. The world is your oyster.

Practical Assignments

1. Describe the principles of three leading companies in the marketplace today. What does their ethos reveal to you?

2. Describe in detail how you intend to implement the principle of "Life is an opportunity to serve people" in your life.

3. List and develop new ideas to improve the lives of people around you. Include action plans for implementation.

4. Were there instances in your life when you refused to serve people? What was the result? Draw conclusions for the future.

Chapter 6

THE POWER
OF PERSUASION

Chapter 6
THE POWER
OF PERSUASION

The Law of the Universe

In the previous chapter, we addressed the value of service to people and its role in relation to creating opportunities. In this chapter, we will examine the impact the strength of our beliefs has on our ability to identify and use opportunities. It is important to understand that the universe and our subconscious mind cannot distinguish the good from the bad. Fear and enthusiasm are perceived on the same level as they are both energies. What we invest energy in is what will manifest in our reality. Therefore, it is important we generate positive energy for what we want, and dispel negative energy – fear, anxiety, etc., so that our reality does not manifest negativity. Think about it – life is like a catalogue from which you can choose whatever you want, so concentrate your energy on getting what you want rather than what you do not want from the catalogue of life. Between man and the universe, there is a flexible dynamic, which takes wisdom to master. Consider the universe as just a device for illustrating our ideas, drawing whatever we say or put our focus and energy on.

Let's look at the law of attraction. According to this law, "like attracts like". The philosophy behind this is that by focusing on positive or negative thoughts a person brings positive or negative experiences into existence. This belief is based upon the idea that people and their thoughts are both made from "pure energy", and the belief that like energy attracts like energy. Our consciousness is able to stimulate heaven or hell and manifest our dominating thoughts into reality. The idea is that the universe is serving you what you order: your waiter is the energy you give to your beliefs and your thoughts become the vehicle which transform into the energy which is delivered to the universe. Everything that happens in our lives, the presence or absence of chance and opportunity, is our sole responsibility. Your health, relationships, finances and so on are all determined and developed by your thoughts. Your position in life has nothing to do with the economic situation in the country, the government or political party in power. Not even the level of education you have received has anything to do with your current condition; even the behaviour of your employer or past events in your life have no bearing on who you are today. The crux of who you are is born out of what you choose to believe. All opportunities are available to you, awaiting your order through the energy your beliefs transmit to the universe to create the life you ordered. Use your energy to positively attract the reality that will enrich your life.

We live in a world of faith and free will. **Faith is the ability to form reality.** The origin of any business starts with an idea. In fact, the origin of anything that becomes reality is an idea. You must first conceive it in your mind, and take action to make it a reality. Your faith in the idea that originated from your mind is the catalyst that will drive your actions to convert into reality. You can use faith to grasp your idea from your subconscious. If you believe and take the time to work on your idea, you will be successful. The belief must be rooted deep in your heart, and if you work with all you have, that idea will certainly come into being, into reality. This powerful essence of faith is creation. Faith must be applied with work – this is evident in the characters of all successful people. It is also the first requirement needed in rightly seeking and seizing opportunities.

Faith must be applied wisely in order to get the best outcome. It is a powerful double-edged sword; on the one hand it will help you grow, and on the other it can paralyse you if applied wrongly. Faith can enrich you, but it's also capable of plunging you into the mire of hopeless poverty. Whatever tools you have acquired in life – be it education, social status or money – without faith they will have no result.

As children we are a product of our parents' DNA and the environment in which we develop. The nature vs nurture debate asks whether a person's development is predisposed by his DNA or if individual inclinations influenced by life experiences and the environment make the difference. It is important to examine the belief system we inherit from our parents and our environment. It is our responsibility to do this in order to achieve a life of purpose. If we fail to create our own belief system, it is likely we will be conducting our life based on the influence of our parents, others and the environment. Do not allow your perception of the world to be based on other people's interpretations as you are free to decide what your world should be. As an adult, you can create your nature vs nurture belief to match your desire and reality. Perception of the world can be according to how you want your world to manifest. You can start by renewing and transforming your mind. The quality of your mind will determine your ability to receive quality opportunities and convert those opportunities to success. Your configuration of who you are will produce the ability to connect with opportunities. If you are configured internally to think that opportunities are difficult to acquire or are of little use, your reality will create evidence to support your belief; the universe will obey you and manifest the result of your configuration to be your reality. In order to change your reality, start from within.

Our Achilles Heel Is A State Of Mind

People love to act disappointed. Even though we plan our affairs with the mind-set that it "either works or it doesn't", we become disappointed when the plan ends with the "not working" even though that was in our plan. Why? People repeatedly accept defeat even before they set out to execute their plan. You must remember that our reality is the sum total of our thoughts. You must use your thoughts to create the best life for yourself. Eliminate the negative attitude of believing that you are unlucky, that things don't work well for you or that the chance of success is 50:50. You are in control of your thoughts and hence your life, so order what you want from the universe, believing with all your might that you will get what you ordered. Discard negative thoughts and fill your mind with the positive reality you desire. Opportunities slip away from under our noses every day. Living in anger, irritation, frustration, resentment and bitterness will rob you of the opportunities around you. If you are familiar with these feelings, it means that you have created your script of being. Your pattern of behaviour and responses to a given situation will manifest your belief. Start writing a new script to support a fruitful, purposeful and successful reality.

When people say, "I was unlucky," they assume they did everything possible, but that something higher prevented them from achieving their goal. They are right, but the higher source only presented them with what they requested. They were prevented by something, but that something was created by them; it was their instruction that was delivered by the universe. **Faith in failure creates failure.** We are creators, and we create our world with our faith, beliefs and ideas. It is interesting to observe how people can believe something is possible but yet that same thing is not possible for them. They say "Yes, I know it's possible, but not for me…" and to convince themselves of the correctness of this conclusion, they further convince themselves that they have "No money, and not enough time" or "I have a family to feed" and the deception goes on and on. To benefit from a successful outcome you must accept that if you can conceive it in your mind, it is a possibility and it can be created by you. They sincerely believe that something cannot be done but they don't understand the difference between facts and fictions, rendering a person to live a life of mediocrity, setbacks and defeats.

The harder you think it is to achieve any result, the harder it will be, as your thoughts become your reality. Do you ever wonder how some people achieve a goal, while others struggle with the same goal? A businessman knows business does not depend on the goods or services alone, it greatly depends on the individual selling the products or services. I am sure you have heard the saying "People buy people". Other than the economic forces of supply and demand, the reason why one person can sell trash and be successful while the other tries to sell gold and fails is because of what you have put inside of you, your beliefs. Remember what becomes reality in your world is what you created from the inside. If you are insecure and hopeless about your product or your services, that is what people will see. Nobody will willingly buy pessimism as remember, people buy people. Be what you want to see in others. Look closer at your life, and you will observe how your reality depends on how you treat yourself. Mark 12:31 says "love your neighbour as thy self". This commandment is not a coincidence, it is a vital key to successful living.

Connecting Thoughts and Character

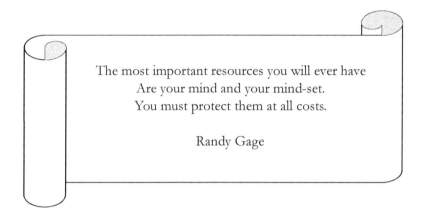

The most important resources you will ever have
Are your mind and your mind-set.
You must protect them at all costs.

Randy Gage

An elderly man was sitting by an oasis at the entrance to a Middle Eastern city. A young man came up to him and their conversation was as follows:

Young man – *I've never been here. What kind of people live in this city?*

The elderly man answered him with a question:

Elderly man – *What kind of people are in the city you came from?*

Young man – *They are selfish and evil people, that's why I left.*

Elderly man – *Here you will meet exactly the same people.*

A little later, another man approached the place and asked the same question:

Another man – *I just arrived. Tell me, old man, what kind of people live in this city?*

The elderly man answered the same:

Elderly man – *Tell me, son, how did the people behave in the town where you came from?*

Another man – *Oh, they are kind, hospitable and noble souls. I left a lot of friends there, and it was hard to part with them.*

Elderly man – *You will find the same here.*

A farmer who was watering his camels heard both dialogues. And as soon as the second man walked away, he turned to the old man, disapprovingly.

Farmer – *How can you give two people two completely different answers to the same question?*

Elderly man – *My son, everyone wears his world in his heart. Those who in the past have not found anything good in those places where they came from will certainly not find anything here. On the contrary, the same one who had friends in another city, here too, will find true and loyal friends. For, you see, the people around us become what we find in them.*

This story is a parable and a simple lesson about life as we know it. The key lesson here is that whatever we believe, we create. We carry our world along with us everywhere we go and it is what we make of it. Our world is what it is because we make it that way. Any mental attempt to describe our world will create it. Your belief of anyone or anything is what will become reality. Everyone sees through the prism of their own unique experience and this is their reality. External circumstances and what surrounds us in life are directly related to our internal state.

Protecting your Thoughts

This story illustrates another lesson. Some frogs decided to organise a race, with a goal of climbing to the top of a tower. On the day of the competition there were many spectators watching and laughing at the contestants for the mammoth task they were about to embark on. As the competition began, frog contestants hurried forward to conquer the tower. None of the spectators believed the frogs would be able to climb to the top. The spectators shouted all manner of comments – it is impossible! They will never get to the top! No chance!

With this negative roar from the spectators, one after the other the frogs suddenly began to fall from the tower as they were climbing. Some would fall rise and continue only to fall again. The crowd continued to yell doubt and impossibility. Frog after frog continued to fall from exhaustion. However, there was one particular frog, climbing non-stop higher and higher until he achieved the finishing height. This frog climbed to the end and won the race.

At the end of the competition the exceptional frog who had put in maximum effort and reached the top of the tower was asked how he did it. Everyone wanted to know how he was able to climb to the end when other frogs had failed. One of the participants of the competition asked the frog, where did you find the strength? It turns out, the winner was deaf! This doesn't mean you have to be deaf in order to win a race or be successful in life. It is about what you believe, what you listen to and accept to be your reality.

The moral of this story is to be mindful of the voice you listen to; never listen to the "naysayers" – you must turn a deaf ear to those or that which is contrary to your goal. If you hear, you do not have to listen to or believe the negativity. Pessimism will destroy your deepest ambitions if you let it. If you allow people to comment on or dictate your life, you will never realise your strength and purpose.

"The most important resources for us as humans are consciousness and attitude," – Randy Gage. We must protect these two attributes with diligence, as our life depends on it. To protect your mind from such negative interference, first you need to analyse your social circle and cut off the naysayers, whiners and pessimists in your life. Instead find like-minded optimists who believe in success as much as you do. It is easier to get to the top with like-minded people, who believe in strengthening their circle.

The next key consideration to success is to reject the "old world". Regardless of how it was created, this is the subconscious conditioning of your environment or the unproductive influences of your upbringing by parents, family, guardians or friends. It is any past experience that does not support your goal or future aspirations.

In order to develop your strengths and achieve success, you must:

• Identify the problem areas in your thinking, and fix them

• Re-programme your thinking to positive thoughts, applied with positive attitude

- Change your beliefs, programme yourself with the right beliefs and act on your goals

- Change your environment

- Don't give up on your dreams

- Do not accept pessimism from yourself and others

- Believe in yourself and your strength

- Believe in God who has already given you the ability to succeed

- Have a heart of gratitude

As you make these changes you must also cultivate awareness of the laws of the universe and have confidence in the innate talents and abilities that fate generously awards. Believe in your God-given ability, that what you can conceive, you can achieve. YOU CAN DO ALL THINGS! "I can do all things through Christ who strengthens me," says Philippians 4:13. Remember the power of words. "The tongue has the power of life and death, and those who love it will eat its fruit" –Proverbs 18:21. Do not allow others to sow seeds of doubt in your heart.

In this chapter we addressed the influence of our beliefs on our lives, which converts to our ability to respond to opportunities. It is clear that much of our success or failure is dependent on the strength of our convictions. We must pay optimal attention to our thoughts and convictions which become our reality.

Golden Nuggets

1. The universe and our subconscious mind cannot distinguish good from evil; both fear and faith are perceived the same way.

2. It is important to focus our energy on the positive things we want to happen in our lives.

3. We attract what we think; the circumstances and the people around us confirm the dominant images in our head.

4. Faith is the ability to shape reality. Faith in failure will create failure, Faith in success creates success.

5. Your level and quality of opportunity is in direct correlation to your awareness. External circumstances and what surrounds you in life are directly related to your internal state.

6. To change something in reality, the change starts within.

7. Everything in your life depends on how you see yourself, which results in how you treat yourself.

8. Never listen to naysayers, their pessimism will hold you back and diminish your dreams.

9. Your most vital resource is your consciousness and attitude. Consciously order what you want to see in your reality, and the universe will serve you according to your dominant thoughts.

Self-Examination Test

1. What do you spend most of your time thinking about?

a) I constantly worry about what is going to happen to me – 0 points;

b) Most of the time my mind is full of troubles and worries – 1 point;

c) In most cases I have a positive attitude – 3 points;

d) I am full of positive expectations from life and feelings of joy and peace – 4 points.

2. Which of the statement below best describes your attitude to life?

a) I am just a grain of sand in this world, tossed around by a storm by accident – 0 points;

b) If not for the unjust circumstances around me, I would be living much better – 1 point.

c) I often encounter attempts that prevent me from achieving what I want – 2 points;

d) I fully accept responsibility for my life; my life, my rules – 4 points.

3. Do you think that people usually do not understand you?

a) Yes! That is why they are always against me – 0 points;

b) Quite often – 1 point;

c) Rarely – 2 points;

d) That never happens, I make myself clear – 4 points.

4. Are you optimistic about life?

a) Optimism is being naive – 0 points;

b) Not really – 1 point;

c) I try to be optimistic most of the time – 2 points;

d) Yes – 4 points.

5. What would you consider joy?

a) Nothing – 0 points;

b) Evidence that humans are doing well – 1 point;

c) Help during difficult times – 3 points;

d) The thought of learning something new – 4 points.

Test Results

Up to 4 Points – You are the root of your problem. You believe life only has a few opportunities and you are excluded from them. A full overhaul of your belief system is urgently needed. You must change your attitude and perceptions. Start by consciously learning to develop a positive attitude and view of the world around you. Be gracious for the things you have, for the people around you and, most importantly, cultivate a positive attitude towards yourself. Continue to read this book and you will benefit from the lesson in each chapter. Carefully work through the practical exercises and success is sure to be yours.

5–8 Points – Your attitude towards life prevents you from making the most of the opportunities in your path. You are misusing the events in your life that could give you the opportunities you need to attain success. You must continue to read this book, completing the practical assessments and gaining a better understanding of how to change for the better.

9–12 Points – Your score is not bad, but it could be better! You have the self-confidence and the ability to control your beliefs and protect your mind from destructive and negative thoughts. Continue to develop your ability to attract the life you want. This book will help you.

13–16 Points – Congratulations! You know what you want and you have the right approach to identify opportunities around you. Few things can knock you off track. Create a value chain by teaching others the skills you have mastered so well. Share your optimism with the people around you.

Practical Assignments

1. **Think about what shaped your view of the world, analyse the influences in your life. Identify** what false or negative attitudes and views you have absorbed, identify from whom. Once identified, start the process of detox.

2. **Analyse how you think about your future.** Consciously establish your life. How would you start to create the life you want? How would you create

a "new world" for yourself? Develop what you have learned from this book, and remember your ideas of the future must align with your dominant thoughts.

3. **Analyse the destructive beliefs in your life.** Identify the source of these beliefs or the opinions that affect your goals and chances. Only you have the power to change your world.

4. **Develop methods to protect your consciousness.** What will you do in order to get rid of the naysayers and destructive beliefs? Develop new positive beliefs and effect your reality for the better.

5. **Examine and analyse the biographies of five great men or women of our time.** What beliefs did they have about themselves that made them great? List ten lessons you learnt from these great men and women.

Chapter 7.

THE GAME OF THE LAKE OF JOY

Chapter 7.
THE GAME OF THE LAKE OF JOY

In the previous chapter we covered values and examples of the power of beliefs and the effect on our reality. This chapter gives you a scenario to help you to understand hindrances to your success. Your response to this scenario game will give you vital information on how your beliefs drive your response to opportunities.

The scenario – you discover a unique lake with multiple layers. The top layer is made up of plain water, it has a different combination of water in each layer as it gets deeper. A regular top, with magical depth. This lake is not for swimming in; you must dive in to obtain its essence. The essence is buried deep down in the lake. At the bottom of the lake you are certain to receive luck, wisdom and perfect health. Just by diving through all the layers you are guaranteed a substantial amount of money. The deeper you go, the better your life will be, and it will solve any problem. Participating in the journey to the deep end of this lake will give you enlightenment, wisdom, youthfulness and stamina. Someone has confirmed the validity of the promises of this lake to you.

The Rules of the Game

Access to the lake is open to all, there is no limit to the number that can come at a time. As the lake is a magical lake it will accommodate any number of people at the same time. This lake is located on the other side of the earth from your current location. To locate the lake, you take a globe and identify the opposite point from your current location. Your route to the lake will be a journey to the other side of your current location. Once you make the journey you are guaranteed to find this magical lake. Even if your opposite side of the earth is the centre of New York City, you will find the lake. Once you arrive at the magical lake and dive in, the magical layers and essence will activate seven seconds after you run out of air in your lungs. As an example, if you can last 20 seconds underwater, in order to reach the magical layer, you have to hold your breath for another seven seconds, totalling 27 seconds. Realistically you need to have an extra 15 seconds of breath, and overall, 35 seconds. In order to reach the magical layer of water, you must overcome the "point of no return". The point of no return is the deep in the lake when you have to make a decision either to:

A. Swim forward, but then you are guaranteed not to have enough air to ascend.

B. Turn around and start to swim upward, having just enough air to surface.

If you decide to go to the end of the magical layer you will sail back with a fresh supply of air. In this layer, there is a chance to breathe, it's magic.

You need to note that your time allowance will increase if at the moment you learned about the lake, you were capable of being underwater for 20 seconds. If after training to develop better underwater staying power you increase your time to 40 seconds, your point of no return will change to 30 seconds. 10 seconds is quite enough to ascend. But if you push on, deep into the lake at 32 seconds, you will not have enough oxygen to ascend, you will drown, because you are deep in ordinary water.

Note:

1. Unlimited number of dives allowed.

2. For each new dive you must go back to your original location and start the journey to the lake again.

3. No tools allowed, you must dive into the lake unaided.

Now answer these questions. Would you go to this lake? When? Under what circumstances? Take this game as an opportunity to reflect on how you would respond to the scenario and the questions above. Your conclusion should help you to identify your strengths and weaknesses and develop a plan for successful living.

Responding to Opportunities

In the above lake scenario, the first thing that might stop you is disbelief of the existence of this magical lake. Even if you were shown a video of the lake, you would still have your doubts. In life people often miss opportunities just because they do not believe in the possibility. In fact, they may even believe it could happen for others but not for them. The question is, what do you believe?

Consider the following example: a person has a dream to travel around the world. As we have learned in previous chapters, there are two categories of people in relation to opportunities. The first category consists of approximately 95% of the world's population. They will find many reasons preventing them from executing their dream to travel around the world. The second category consists of only 5% of the world's population. This group of people are positive, they are ambitious, adventurous and in control of their lives. Although they may have many reasons preventing their dreams from happening, their focus will be on what they can do to achieve their dreams.

The group with the 95% of the population enjoys exchanging the stories of their woes with others in this category. They debate their problems and compete on who has the bigger problem in life. It's easy to fall into this trap because there are more people in the world in this category, they have a mundane mind-set and are not willing to grow. To succeed in life and seize each opportunity you must detach yourself from the mediocre way of thinking and turn your life to reflect desire and attain fulfilment.

• Change "I have no money" to "Where can I get money?" The answer is obvious: "Go earn it" – but it will require effort.

• Change "I have no time" to "How can I make the time?" – Plan your day and spend less time on frivolous things. Stop watching others live their dreams, while you bury yours. Eliminate pointless engagements with time spent watching television and on social media, unless they are helping you to achieve success and realise your dreams.

- Change "I do not have the ability" to "Where can I learn how to do this?" – With the advent of technology you can self-educate. Read books, go to seminars and trainings in the area of your interest.

There are no magic pills to life. If you believe and say, "I do not have," then you never will, until you change your mind; believe and profess what you want. Once you change your words to "How can I get it?" answers will start to pop up everywhere. Pay attention and take action as opportunities arise.

Thinking out loud here, why is it that the 95% category are not emulating the 5% of people that dare to believe in themselves and the opportunities life offers? This is an age-old question and we must look within ourselves for the answer. However, it is more important to take the actions necessary to join the 5%, than merely providing the answer. The antidote is to believe, your belief will drive your action and result in the life you create. Those in the category of the 5% start with the foundation of faith in the impossibility.

It is evident that by our own will, we neglect to explore opportunity that is life. Nobody is to blame; we possess the power to claim what we want from life. Your life, your destiny is in your hands. Your lifestyle, your daily routine must consciously include identifying opportunities, making the effort and using the opportunity as a stepping stone to achieve purpose and a successful life.

The fact remains, if a person passionately strives for something, makes the right choice no matter how difficult it may be, the situation will eventually bow to the person who is persistent. Your story depends on you, you are the writer of your destiny, so take the pen to paper – life – and write yourself a successful reality.

Illusion or a Reality?

Let's go back to the lake. Envisage you made the decision to go to the lake, even borrowed money for the journey. You arrived to discover there is no lake. How would you feel? What would be your prevailing thought at the turnout of events? Would it be, "I knew it, I cannot trust anyone," or "Well, there is no lake, but at least I made the journey, I believe in myself and my ability to complete the tasks set for the lake"? Would you allow the outcome of the journey to turn you into a pessimist or an optimist? The choice is yours, but choose wisely.

This tells us that a lot depends on our perception of reality. Remember the chapter in which we examined the strength of our convictions – life is not what it is, life is what you make it. Everything depends on our perception; we have the power of interpretation, to convert life to what we want it to be.

Some people choose to live in illusion. So when their illusions are broken and they are faced with reality, stress and depression set in. Indeed, reality differs from illusion; the disparity between reality and illusion creates the pain of an unfulfilled life. Even at this desperate point, there is always an opportunity to make a choice, always another offering from life to conceive and create success for the future.

1. **Identify your reality.** Many people leave in illusion and are not able to separate illusion from reality. You must make the decision to be true to yourself, by identifying facts from fiction and knowing your belief drives your action. Your ability to seek and know the truth will enable you to use failure as a tool and embrace opportunities. Accepting reality means giving up deception and boldly journeying through life's opportunities. Choose the value system that complements your goal. You must master self-awareness and critically analyse your environment.

2. **Dispel any myths.** Your avoidance of the realities of life will not change the truth or work in your favour. You must embrace the reality you created and

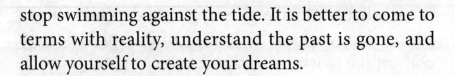

stop swimming against the tide. It is better to come to terms with reality, understand the past is gone, and allow yourself to create your dreams.

The Factor of Time

Anyone can dive, but the magic water layer begins seven seconds after you run out of air. This means that if you can hold your breath underwater for 20 seconds, in order to reach the magical layer, you must not only survive 27 seconds, but also actively swim further down to the depth of the lake. In order to develop your lungs and survive underwater as required, you have to train for at least six months by practising in the pool three times a week for 45 minutes. Do you have what it takes?

The magic lake scenario summarises our life here on earth. In order to realise the essence of life we are required to take part and take action. We are created to be a solution. The problems you invest your time in to solve decide your prominence in life. The solution to a problem is you. Make it your goal to be a solution; your greatness is hidden in the problems you solve and through solving problems you will surely unlock opportunities in life.

If you really want to change your life for the better, you are seriously ready to embark on the journey of success and you must do what it takes by giving your best. Start by identifying problems then find the solution. As in the lake scenario, if you were to give yourself a fighting chance to complete the requirements, you will find the time to train your lungs in the pool three times a week so that you can withstand the strain of the task ahead. Most people struggle with sustained effort in one direction, they lose focus and give up. Study any great athlete and you will discover the level of work they have put into their craft to become great. The time and effort invested will be in direct correlation to the level of their success. Do what you need to do in order to realise your dream. Neglecting to take the action necessary to achieve your dreams will leave you void and unfulfilled. It is not enough to be average; living a life just to satisfy yourself and your instincts is mediocre, you are created for much more. We must add value to ourselves and to others: devaluing our lives by choosing a lesser dream because we are unwilling to do what it takes is a waste of time. Choose worthy goals for yourself and invest your time and efforts on solving problems.

Reasons for Success and Failures in Life

Go back to the lake scenario – this time you have arrived at the lake and there are thousands of people on the shore. Some standing staring at the water, some dive straight in, some already make an attempt but surface disillusioned. Most people are disappointed, and it shows on their faces. Only a few emerge satisfied with a smile; they successfully proceeded to the magical layer. Others stand envious of those who did all that was required to achieve success. This scenario exemplifies our life on earth. Some do all it takes to live a life of purpose and fulfilment, others just complain and do nothing to affect their destiny, and some are envious of those who seized opportunities.

Only 5% of the people at the lake reach the magic layer, and the rest are left with nothing. Now you do the maths: 100% of people learned about the lake, 5% of the 100% accepted the challenge. Of this 5% only another 5% reach the promised layers. In a sample of 1000 people, this equates to 50 people who took the challenge and of the 50, 2.5 people dived and reached the magic layer. In the magical lake scenario and the numbers is the true reality of life. Most people fail to grab opportunity and, even worse, fail to take the action required to convert opportunities.

Consider the excuses people who failed at the lake were making. The negative self-talk, lack of focus, disbelief, lack of vision, condemnation – the list goes on. What are your excuses? Lessons learnt! Develop a strong network in which you can encourage one another. Consider every problem as an opportunity to be the solution. Invest your time in preparing for opportunity.

Live Life as a Constant Movement towards Your Goals

Life is predictable. Although it has many ups and downs, we are the architects of our lives. Allowing obstacles to push you to give up on your dreams in not a wise choice. The exchange for a fulfilling life are time and effort. The life you live now was once a dream, an idea someone invested time and effort in converting to reality. Life has many layers of dreams that were once just an idea; someone had to dive in to create the reality you live now. By not working on your dreams, you are rejecting opportunities and the vision of future success. Everything that surrounds us is inspiration to inform us of how life evolves. Nothing is eternal, today's new inventions will cease to impress tomorrow.

Dream big as you pursue your dreams and you will gain the motivation for greater height. When you embark on a journey to achieve your dreams, there is no better motivation – the physical response to achievement is invaluable. Your dream propels your body to generate energy. This is a principle of success – if you think about it, much like the muscles in the body, the more you use it the stronger it is. Same is true of life without a dream: without purpose it deteriorates and eventually dies.

A man walks towards his goal like a sedge of cranes flying south. He pulls back and forth; he knows how good he will feel when he reaches his destination. Yes, death is inevitable, we will all go someday, but rather than dying empty, at least know you gave it your all and achieved purpose.

Strive towards your dreams daily

What are the things that can prevent us from achieving our dreams and taking advantage of opportunities?

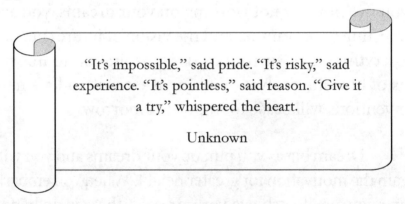

"It's impossible," said pride. "It's risky," said experience. "It's pointless," said reason. "Give it a try," whispered the heart.

Unknown

Dos and don'ts

Don't be deterred by the arguments of reason, with all its logic trying to convince you that your dreams are impossible. How many things were thought impossible until they were done and became reality?

Do not let the past stop you; memory of past failures should not be entertained. Remind yourself that this is a new endeavour.

Do away with your pride. Pride is a bad counsellor, it discourages you from opportunities. "Whoever looks for millions, rarely finds them, but someone who is not looking for them – never finds them," said Honoré de Balzac, a French writer, one of the founders of realism in European literature.

Strive to follow your dreams. Have a goal and work towards it daily; it will help you to develop the awareness to identify opportunities and achieve success.

Dreams are expressed in our desires and are demonstrated in the willingness to invest time and effort for them to come to fruition. They are the images of thought with strong positive emotions.

Doubters will say it's impossible, it's not for you. But if this is your dream, it is not for others to understand, it is in fact impossible for others to understand because they did not receive the vision.

"Our doubts are traitors, and make us lose the good that we might oft win, by fearing to attempt," said William Shakespeare, English poet and playwright, considered the greatest English language writer and one of the best playwrights in the world.

Most importantly, there are limitless opportunities in the world to support your dream. Your ability to see and use them depends on your desire and drive. "Those who firmly believe in the direction of their desires and dare to live their dreams inevitably meet success," said Henry David Thoreau, American writer, thinker, naturalist and public figure.

Dreams and visions help us create our future. Mark Twain, an American writer, journalist and social activist, supposedly wrote: "Twenty years from now you will be more disappointed by the things that you didn't do than by the ones you did. So throw off the bowlines. Sail away from the safe harbour. Catch the trade winds in your sails. Explore! Dream! Discover!"

Golden Nuggets

1. In life, people often miss opportunities because they do not believe in the possibility of the existence of opportunities.

2. If your tomorrow is not better than your today, remember you are in control.

3. It is possible to implement every idea; dreams do become reality.

4. Those who believe in illusion neglect reality at their peril.

5. You exist as a solution to a problem. Be the solution that you are created to be.

6. Life is a constant movement, move in the direction of your dreams.

7. Failing to dream is one way to kill yourself.

8. Dream big, ignite your power and extend your life span.

9. A man will be satisfied with his life only when he realises that these dreams are significant not only for him but for the benefit of many.

10. Our dreams and visions are the foundations to create the future.

Self-Examination Test

1. Are you ready to dive into the enchanted lake and hold your breath, go forward into the magic layer, breaking the point of no return?

a) I would not even go to find the lake. It is definitely a trap! – 0 points;

b) It is too risky, and what if it is all made up? – 1 point;

c) Oh, I would very much like to, developing my stamina ahead of time – 2 points;

d) I certainly want to take the chance – 4 points.

2. How do you respond to people who have achieved success?

a) They are arrogant, know it all – 0 points;

b) They think life revolves around them. I find them annoying – 1 point;

c) It's good to see someone doing well. Hopefully, I will join them someday – 3 points;

d) We are on the same team, like attracts like – 4 points.

3. How do you usually respond when you get a chance?

a) What chance? – 0 points;

b) Usually I don't have enough time or money to take any chances – 1 point

c) I do not always succeed in taking chances but I will go for it – 2 points;

d) I find all possible ways to take advantage of every opportunity – 4 points.

e) Ч

4. How do you usually spend time with your friends?

a) We spend time to discuss how difficult life is – 0 points;

b) Brag to each other, complain about our problems, and we will not rest until we feel better about ourselves – 1 point;

c) We spend a lot of time partying/clubbing, and consuming the fun things in life – 2 points;

d) We only talk about our goals and how to accomplish them – 4 points.

5. Are you ready for many months of training to achieve the desired result?

a) Are you crazy! I need to take care of myself – 0 points;

b) No. I don't have enough strength – 1 point;

c) I often begin with zeal and passion, but then my aspirations fade – 3 points;

d) I will give all my time and effort to achieve my goals – 4 points.

Test Results

Up to 4 Points – You are limiting your success rate by your belief systems. It is not too late for you to develop the qualities required to be open to opportunities. Start by consciously saying yes to life, rejecting pessimism and focusing your energy on being positive in every situation, even in problematic ones. Cultivate an attitude that sees the best in every situation. Follow the guidance in this book and you will be amazed how your life will change for the better. You have already begun the journey to your best self.

5–8 Points – Your answers have revealed lapses in your ability to recognise opportunities. Lucky for you, the fact that you are reading this book is an opportunity in itself. Use this book as a tool to rid you of the hindrances preventing you from life's opportunities. Study the facts and complete the practical assessments, these will help you to develop the skills and knowledge needed to be able to identify opportunities and positively impact your reality.

9–12 Points – You are not in a bad place. You can identify some aspects of life's opportunities, but you can do much better. Your development is critical at this stage, so start to take charge of your life, believe in yourself and your dreams. Boldly acknowledge and work on your dreams until they become reality. You are the architect of your own life.

13–16 Points: Well done! You already possess what it takes. Nothing can stop you now. You have and will continue to achieve every success with the mind-set evident from your answers. Identifying opportunities is second nature to you, so why don't you help others to develop their ability? Continue to dive through the layers of life, as with your attitude to life you can never go unnoticed. The world is your oyster – you are in a position to take the opportunities that life has to offer.

Practical Assignments

1. **Based on the "Magic Lake" game, answer the following questions:** Would you go to the lake? When would you go? How would you make the journey? What is the reason for your decision?

2. **It is necessary to dive through the "point of no return".** Have you had a point of no return in your life experiences? How did you handle this stage? What was the outcome of your experience?

3. **Are you open to new ideas, opinions and suggestions?** What is your typical reaction to change? Do you welcome change or struggle with it? What have

you done about your response to change? What areas do you want to develop in order to respond appropriately to change?

4. **How have you focused your efforts to implement your long term goals?** What has prevented you from achieving your goals? Develop a plan and strategy to eliminate your drawbacks.

5. **Back to the lake scenario, the crowd by the lake.** Identify who you are in the crowd, identify who you would associate with.

6. **What are your dreams?** How do you seek to achieve your dreams? What is your purpose on earth? What is keeping you alive?

Chapter 8

YOU WASTE YOUR LIFE WHEN YOU LET OPPORTUNITIES SLIP

Chapter 8
YOU WASTE YOUR LIFE WHEN YOU LET OPPORTUNITIES SLIP

Great opportunities come to all, but many
Are not even aware that they met them.

William Dunning

A religious man was in a village. One day it rained heavily and the whole village was flooded. The religious man climbed on a roof and sat praying for help so that he would not drown. Along came a man in a boat, who shouted to the religious man on the roof to jump on board with him.

"No, God will help me," said the religious man.

The water rose higher and a second boat came by

"Jump in, the water is rising!" said the man in the boat.

"No thank you, God will help me," said the religious man again.

By now the water had risen to the religious man's neck. Finally, a helicopter flew by and the pilot shouted, "Get in, there is no other way out, you will die if you don't get in the helicopter now!"

The religious man answered in his usual response, "No God will help me."

The religious man eventually drowned. He appeared before God and asked,

"Why didn't you save me God? I relied on you."

God replied, "I sent multiple offers of help to you, but you failed to heed to my help."

Consider the moral of this story – could you be the religious man in the story?

In earlier parts of this book we have examined opportunities from various angles: what are the opportunities in our lives, why we often do not recognise opportunities, and how to respond to them. We are now going to focus on what to do with opportunities once they have been identified – the right questions and the solution we are created to be.

It is common that when in search of what we believe to be the best, we fail to notice the opportunities in our path. **Not missing opportunities means seeing them for what they are. We must always be mindful** that opportunities are available to all of us, but many of us are blind to the opportunities around us. This is principally because we have not developed the skills necessary for seeking and seizing opportunities.

"Destiny is not a matter of chance. It is a matter of choice. It is not a thing to be waited for, it is a thing to be achieved," said William Jennings Bryan, an American orator and politician from Nebraska, and a dominant force in the populist wing of the Democratic Party. This should inspire us to do our part in planning for opportunities. The ball is in our court; it is up to us to make the next move. Once we can identify with facts, we can be sure of fulfilling our purpose. Life completely depends on us for its essence. It is our responsibility to create substance and to convert our dreams to reality. We are the vessels carrying a purpose and destiny which gives life its full meaning. Have you ever considered how your life would have been if you had never missed an opportunity? If you had seized upon every opportunity and executed all the ideas that God had placed in your heart? What would your life be like now?

When God places an idea into your mind, He knows you are capable of delivering, and He provides the resources needed to achieve success. It is your responsibility to act upon the idea until it becomes reality. All of the things we now enjoy in life were once ideas until someone like you took the action and converted it into reality. The things you see now were once ideas; they became reality when someone like you believed and did all it took to bring them into reality. God freely gives many opportunities, and it is our choice to accept them. The decision to accept or neglect these gifts is a choice. Doing nothing is still a choice. When we choose not to explore the ideas given to us and fail to seize the opportunities needed to achieve our goals, we are at a loss with far-reaching consequences on the quality of our lives.

Most people fail to identify opportunities because they are in the form of a problem, difficulty or trouble. The key is to recognise your superiority as a solution to any problem. Once you know you are created as a solution, you will always identify a problem for what it is – an opportunity. Take the bull by the horns and open the floodgate of opportunities. Here are some key considerations when identifying opportunities:

- Opportunities do not always appear desirable; a diamond in is original state is not desirable until it is refined.

- Don't be too quick to dismiss anyone or anything. Do your research and ask lots of questions.

- Before you conclude that you "can't", rephrase to How? What do I need?

- Opportunities do not always fit into our stereotypes and beliefs. Identify the source of your belief system – who is in charge of your life?

- Be flexible; the universe has more to offer than you can ever imagine.

- If it comes to you, your consciousness, it is yours for the taking. The universe does not discriminate, take action to see it to fruition.

Let's look at what we need to do in order to make use of opportunities, as intended by God. These are principles you must master in order to succeed.

Opportunities May Arrive in any Form – Toughness and Difficulty are common in opportunity

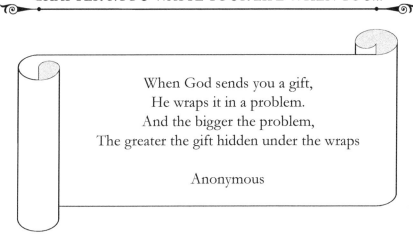

When God sends you a gift,
He wraps it in a problem.
And the bigger the problem,
The greater the gift hidden under the wraps

Anonymous

Do not lose opportunities because they come in the form you don't like. More often than not, in a high percentage of cases, opportunities are disguised as a problem. If we were to describe it in the form of a package, it would be an unpleasant package. Your responsibility is to unravel its essence and make the best use of the content. We must always remember that opportunities and challenges go hand in hand. Prospects usually stem from challenges: problems, crises and difficulties all have hidden opportunities for which you are already equipped to resolve.

The great inventor Thomas Edison nearly lost his hearing at age 14. The likely cause was an infection. One day a fire broke out at a station close to his lab and the conductor threw the young Edison out with his printing press and equipment, literally pulling him by his ears out of the train. This painful experience could have been a tragedy for someone else, but this was not the case for Edison. If you can, envisage the challenges faced by a person already hard of hearing. This gave Edison no reason to remain in obscurity and self-pity. Edison later said his deafness served him well, as during the day he could work without being distracted by background noise and the remaining time he slept like the dead. Can you see the value in the story of Edison? What are the problems or challenges in your life? Can you turn them to your advantage or could others benefit from the experience you gained from the misfortune?

"In the middle of difficulty lies opportunity," said Albert Einstein. In essence, problems are hidden opportunities. It is very rare that opportunities will be obvious and easy to identify; you have to look beyond the obvious to find the treasure in opportunities. The key to a purposeful life is learning to identify opportunities in problems; if you master this you will no longer be afraid because you know that whatever the circumstances, you have a package of opportunities and you will end victorious. You should by now know that problems have value; since opportunities are hidden in problems, the need to embrace problems increases in order to benefit from the treasure they possess.

Your next problem, your next opportunity. The fact is, as you are solving one problem, new problems are generated. This is the key to life, and evidence of the value of problems.

"Life without problems is like school without classes; you are probably not going to learn anything," Anonymous.

If you are not able to solve one problem, there is no excuse not to attempt to solve another. If not this problem, you are equipped to solve many others. We have different abilities, and having the mind-set of a solution provider is pivotal to seizing opportunities. As we solve one problem, we develop the skills and resources to solve more problems along the way. Start the journey by solving one problem at a time and as you do so, doors to success will be inevitable.

"Problems are opportunities for self-development," said Louise Lynn Hay, an American motivational author and founder of Hay House. She has authored several New Thought self-help books, including the 1984 book, *You Can Heal Your Life*.

When you avoid problems, you run away from your destiny. Stop being afraid of problems, stop running away from them. You will find destiny in problems. Most often opportunities come in the form of problems. People who run away from problems are running away from opportunities. If our parents considered the risks and challenges of childbirth, none of us would have been born. Treasures are born from problems. Pregnancy and childbirth often take a toll on a woman's body, their figure is affected, and they may never get their body back to what it was pre-baby. Childbirth is risky to the life of the mother and on her relationships. We accept these risks in the knowledge that it is exchanged for something of value, a new life.

The value of problems to opportunities is endless.

• The greater the opportunity, the greater the problem. The more valuable the opportunity, the more valuable the problem. **You must not reject opportunities because they come as problems.** Don't allow the problems to deter you. If the problems are realistic and not self-inflicted you must address them until you arrive at a solution. Sometimes a woman becomes unexpectedly pregnant, and is not ready to take on the challenges of pregnancy and becoming a mother. In this scenario there are options for the woman to consider: termination, adoption or keeping the child. In all of these options, it is important to note that the greatest opportunity for the woman will be the most enduring option. The option that takes her to sacrifice her life the most will yield the most opportunities for her.

• **Do opportunities exist without problems?** Opportunities without challenges are likely to be deceptions. These have been seen in many high profile Ponzi schemes, tailored to defraud individuals and companies from their hard-earned cash. As the saying goes, "the only free cheese is in the mouse trap," (Randy Gage). Waiting for perfection will result in overlooking the hidden depths of an opportunity, which could improve your life.

• **It is impossible to be inspired by good ideas if you fail to value uniqueness.** You will never have the ideal circumstances – you just have to be determined to take the bull by the horns. THE MULTITUDE OF YOUR PROBLEMS DETERMINE THE MULTITUDE OF YOUR GLORY. **The harder the path, the bigger the success.**

In summary of these chapters, these are the key facts to remember:

• Opportunities are hidden in problems and troubles.

• Fear will paralyse you, so discard fear before it destroys you. Don't be afraid of problems.

• Look for opportunities, look for problems and be the solution.

Opportunities Are Packages Unmarked

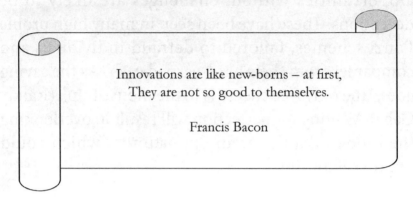

Innovations are like new-borns — at first,
They are not so good to themselves.

Francis Bacon

Andrew and Alina have been friends since high school. They live in the same neighbourhood and spent most of their teenage years together. These two friends' relationship grew stronger through to university and graduation. They were known as the couple most likely to get married first amongst their peers. Although Alina loved Andrew and he loved her too, he was adamant that she lost weight before he made her his wife. This was a thorn in Alina's flesh as she tried desperately to please Andrew so that they could be married and live together as man and wife. Several years passed after their graduation. Alina was unable to lose the weight and eventually Andrew decided it was time they go their separate ways. He had found the girl to satisfy his physical desires. Alina was devastated but she knew there was nothing she could do as Andrew had already proposed to his dream girl.

If Andrew had not focused on the package, on Alina's weight, he would have noticed that at 20 years of age, Alina had other great qualities: she was intelligent, finishing top of her year in university, and was a budding young lawyer with the character of an angel. Alina was sociable and a leader amongst her peers. While Andrew looked at her appearance to judge her unsuitable for him, he lost sight of the awesome potential of this young woman, who cared for him wholeheartedly. Alina found another, a partner at the law firm where she worked. He was able to offer his love and commitment to her. Time passed and Andrew regretted that he missed such a tremendous opportunity, as his relationship with his "dream girl" fizzled out. He was remorseful that he had abandoned a young woman who loved him. After all, the only reason that kept him from being with Alina was his shallow excuse about her weight. Andrew knew Alina was passionate about him and would have given him the world. Appearances are of course important, but priority has to be given to the essence.

Nobody is perfect. We all have our flaws, but the key is to focus on the positives and do our best to improve on our shortcomings. This brings to mind the words of Nikolai Gogol. "Be warned, if you start chasing after views, you'll be left without bread and without views, always think of what is useful and not what is beautiful; beauty will come of its own accord". If you expect a perfect soul-mate, you'll have to wait very long and possibly for the rest of your life. The same applies with opportunities, opportunities do not always come the way you envision.

Opportunities Come in Packages of Discomfort

Opportunities will never come as a complete package. The onus is on us to convert them into successes. We have to take the necessary action to refine opportunities until they are converted into what we desire in reality. We must be able to embrace the inconvenience that comes with opportunities, we must see beyond vision. The saying "Don't throw the baby out with the bath water", means don't discard something valuable along with something undesirable. This popular wisdom is intended as a warning – it should be applied in view of opportunities. Your focus should be on the essence, and at best you should try to negate the negative components that accompany opportunities.

"But he who dares not grasp the thorn should never crave the rose," – Anne Brontë, English novelist and poet. There is no rose without the thorn. The presence of thorns does not diminish the beauty of a rose. Wisdom is to place your hands around the roses without touching the thorns.

In the eyes of an optimist, roses are beautiful flowers with a lovely scent. Conversely, to a pessimist, roses are to be avoided because of the thorns. Although this beautiful flower is one and the same with the thorn, they have opposite effects on our emotions. The same is true of life – two people can be given the same possibilities and one will embrace them while the other despises the chance. The lesson from the rose is that there is beauty in pain. The best we can do is to endure.

Opportunities Demand Sacrifices above the Norm

Several years ago, Valerie lost her source of income. Though she is married, her husband has never been the breadwinner of the family, despite being a very good father to their daughter who is now seven years old. As the burden of providing for the family grew, Valerie thought of nothing but how to provide for her family. Every morning she would leave the house in search of a job, but for a whole year her efforts were in vain.

One year in the approach to Christmas she was offered a job to prepare turkey for a busy family for Christmas. As Valerie completed the task for one family, others were quick to follow suit, asking for her service. She jumped at the chance, although it was a huge challenge to find the money to buy the turkey and prepare in advance of any payment for the produce and service. She thought of the idea to collect part payment from each customer as she took the order. This gave her some capital to purchase the turkeys. She is up in the early hours of the morning collecting payments then goes straight to the farm to purchase her produce. By noon she has prepared and packed the turkeys, taking the rest of the day to deliver to her customers. It was not an easy job for a woman on her own but she persevered.

Year after year, she developed a reputation as the best in the business. Do you remember how she started the business? It was by coincidence; she seized an opportunity that gave her the chance of success. She gained several satisfied customers and developed her business all year round. She started preparing party meals for all occasions. Though Valerie did not have the capital to start the business, she seized the opportunity anyway and the idea of collecting deposits came to her in the process. This is the key to converting an opportunity into a success. You have to embark on the journey by seizing, seeking and engaging with actions, then more information and ideas on how to excel will come to you.

The lesson from Valerie is to perceive and give your best in every situation. **Do not lose opportunities**

because you believe you lack the resources to execute the opportunity. Accept the opportunity and the resources will come as you actively engage to find a solution.

Another lesson from the story of Valerie's business success is her tenacity, intensity, courage and drive to venture into something new. Despite being a woman, and tradition dictating men to be the provider, she did what she had to do for her family. She did not wait around or depend on her husband to be the breadwinner. She was relentless in her pursuit of success.

People observe the world from the perspective of their beliefs, but we must not allow our prejudices to prevent us from opportunities. Our judgments and stereotypes of others can be a hindrance if we are not careful. If not checked, they could cost us in our pursuit of fulfilment.

However, our biases may reflect reality. Beliefs, much like attitudes, are developed over time from childhood. By the time we progress into adulthood, 70% of the information in our brains is set. In this regard, it can be argued that as adults we have formed opinions that are inaccurate about our world. To prevent the disaster of false beliefs, we must constantly examine our thoughts and opinions so we do not miss opportunities.

Despite being a professional and well known in his industry Nicholas, a journalist, was made redundant. The only thing going for Nicholas was his strong desire to change his situation. One morning he called a friend and proposed they start their own advertising business in the city. In his youth Nicolas believed the advertising business was a dirty job, but the current economic climate and his circumstances led him to change his beliefs and adjust to life's demands. Together with his friend Kramer, they gathered up people who were willing to work under their guidance. Within a short time of setting up the business, their company had taken a niche in the advertising market, providing work for hundreds of people. The moral of this story is to identify our stereotypes, develop an understanding of the source of the beliefs and never let them hold us back in our passion to pursue our dreams and make a difference.

In summary:

• There are patterns of thinking that limit and prevent us from taking advantage of opportunities. Identify these patterns and deal with them before they cost you your life.

• If a person decides that he cannot, then he will not! Decide you can and do it.

• Opportunities go beyond limits, unless the limits are set by you.

Opportunities Demand Tenacity

> When one door closes, another opens;
> But we often look so long and so regretfully upon the
> closed door
> That we do not see the one which has opened for us.
>
> Alexander Graham Bell

Peter and Alex had been friends since their university days. By the standards of Soviet society, they had succeeded in life, until suddenly disaster struck with Perestroika *(a political movement for reformation within the Communist Party of the Soviet Union during the 1980s, widely associated with Soviet leader Mikhail Gorbachev and his glasnost ("openness") policy reform).* The existing way of the past years collapsed and turned upside down, and their profession, which had always been considered safe, was no longer needed. The pair, amongst thousands of others in the country, were incapacitated. They thought to themselves, "What shall we do now?"

Alex decided to retrain as a train driver. Concerned his friend was still suffering from the effects of the economic crisis, Alex offered to pay for his friend to retrain. Peter declined Alex's offer. "I am not going to retrain," he said, as he shook his head in disagreement. "I have a PhD. I am a professional with many years of experience". Alex looked at his friend, wondering why he failed to understand that times had changed. Although Alex had the same qualification, he had to retrain in order to make ends meet.

Although they both had good jobs before Perestroika, their previous jobs had become obsolete. The industry in which they worked no longer existed, their specialties becoming irrelevant.

Legendary advertiser and Congressman Bruce Barton survived The Great Depression in America that started in 1929. His company was one of the largest and most successful in the world. Before he reached prominence, he was out of work three times. This was his advice: "The main thing is to continue to stay afloat, be flexible and not be afraid to change the direction of your activities". Flexible people never cling to the past, because they know that it is gone forever and new opportunities are to be seized.

Flexibility is therefore one of the most important qualities of successful people. Flexible people easily adapt to changing circumstances in life. This is especially important at the present time with the development of new technologies and the rapid obsolescence of the old.

The wave of life wipes inflexible people out of its way. To keep up with changing times you must be flexible.

Qualities of a flexible person: open minded, unbiased, not controlled by traditions, fluent in thought and spirit, accepting of change, accepting of criticism and able to turn it around constructively.

Opportunities will be lost if you fail to accept changes. "To improve is to change, to be perfect is to change often," said Winston Churchill, British statesman and Prime Minister of the United Kingdom from 1940 to 1945 and again from 1951 to 1955. If necessary, we must change a hundred times a day if it helps us to achieve our goals.

Wherever there are Opportunities, Risk and Danger Lie Ahead

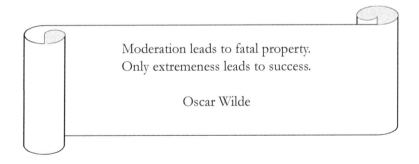

Moderation leads to fatal property.
Only extremeness leads to success.

Oscar Wilde

Opportunity and risk go hand in hand. In finance it is commonly known that the higher the risk profile of an investment, the higher the return. Life itself is a risk, with great opportunities. We navigate through life, uncertain of what tomorrow holds, and that in itself is a risk. Tomorrow is promised to no one, so we must maximise our time, talents and treasures to attain a life that is worthy in the eyes of God. Most of the benefits we enjoy today come with significant risk, especially when they are misused. Think of the ability to drive cars, fly in a plane, or use electricity, computers, social media. In each of these things risks are present but the benefits outweigh the risks. The biggest risk is not taking any risk at all. Failure to take risks is a risk on its own. Taking risks is an essential part of life. "In a rapidly changing world, failure will be guaranteed if risks are not taken," said Mark Zuckerberg, American Internet entrepreneur and co-founder of social networking website Facebook. "If no one ever took risks, Michelangelo would have painted the Sistine Chapel frescoes' floor", said Neil Simon, an American playwright and screenwriter.

Take a look at the biographies of truly wealthy and successful people and you will find one thing in common: they often take risks. Of course, the probability of failure might be high, but they know the probability of success is equally as high. "At the root of every successful enterprise is a once taken courageous decision," said Peter Drucker, an American scientist of

Austrian origin, economist, writer, teacher and one of the most influential theorists of management of the 20th century.

The purpose of mistakes is to show us the direction that will not help us accomplish our goals. When we make mistakes we really do not lose anything, we gain experience and knowledge of how not to do it the next time. People do not become wealthy without risk. Risk does not equate to carelessness; you must do your due diligence and then make a conscious decision to achieve your goals. Risks are often an important element of sound management of capital. "Uncertainty and risk – are the main difficulties and the main business chance," said David Hertz, an American mathematician and analyst. Invest your time wisely and boldly make decisions to take you to the next level in the area of your vocation.

Abandoning opportunities because of the threat of danger would be a tragedy and a loss. One of the most respected US presidents, John F. Kennedy, once said that in Chinese the word "crisis" is written with two characters, one of which is "danger" and the other "opportunity". What does that tell you? People who are afraid of danger and risk are already defeated. In preparation for success we must also prepare for risks.

Risk is the output when you have no guarantee of success. You will eventually overcome the fear of failure once it is replaced by achievements. You will become confident and competent as you move toward goals. "If you want to succeed faster, you must double the frequency of failures. Success lies on the other side of failure," said Thomas J. Watson, legendary American entrepreneur and founder of IBM. Fear of failure can be debilitating and as such it is one of the main hindrances to success. Fear of failure prevents many from even trying at all. "In a moment of indecision act quickly and try to make the first move, even if it is an extra move," – Leo Tolstoy great Russian writer.

The greatest risks and dangers in life are missed opportunities. Sometimes the potential may seem insignificant; other times it might seem huge and overwhelming. The benefit is in taking the steps to overcome your fears. So feel the fear and do it anyway.

In this chapter, we have addressed the issue of missed opportunities and how this equates to a wasted life. We examined seven principles, each of which exposing the myths which hinder success.

Here are some golden truths to remind you of the lessons from this chapter.

Golden Nuggets

1. Problems, crises and troubles have hidden opportunities. Every obstacle and every trouble is a gem equal in magnitude to the opportunity it generates.

2. The greater the problem, the greater the opportunity.

3. Opportunities sometimes come disguised.

4. He who wants to enjoy the beauty of a rose must learn to tolerate its thorns.

5. Opportunities always exceed our natural abilities.

6. Opportunities do not always fit into our stereotypes and beliefs.

7. Never lose opportunities just because they force you to do something you wouldn't normally do.

8. You must be flexible in order to take advantage of opportunities.

9. There are no situations or problems that cannot be solved.

10. Life itself is a risk – opportunity without risk does not exist.

Self-Examination Test

Please take the following test as it will give you an overview of your attitude towards risks and opportunities:

1. How disappointed are you if things do not work out for you?

a. Very disappointed, I sometimes go into a depression when things don't go my way. – 0 points;

b. I'll be nervous and worry, blaming myself for all the wrongs – 1 point;

c. I'll be upset, but in the end, I'll try to convince myself that "everything that is done is for the better", and calm down – 3 points;

d. I'm not upset. I'm sure this is not the end but the beginning of something new in my life – 4 points.

2. Do you agree with the statement "even in times of problems, you will find good"?

b. I don't think so, am I supposed to be happy in times of problems? – 0 points;

c. No, I don't agree – 1 point;

d. It is arguable, but it is possible to find the positive in problems – 2 points;

e. Absolutely, yes – 4 points.

3. Are you ready to give up £100 of your money today, to gain £1,000 tomorrow?

c. A bird in the hand is better than two in the bush – 0 points;

d. Scary! It could be a scam, when will I get the £1000? – 1 point;

e. Maybe – 2 points;

f. Why not? – 4 points.

4. You were supposed to meet with partner, but he or she called to cancel. What would you do?

a. Go home and sulk – 0 points;

b. Return home and make myself busy with household chores – 1 point;

c. It is not the end of the world, "I will get over it" – 3 points;

d. I will do something productive with my time. – 4 points.

Test Results

Up to 4 Points – You are prone to missing opportunities because you are afraid to take risks. Although you may be getting on with life, problems and difficulties cause you to panic and shut down. Your beliefs are based on negative stereotypes, hence your pessimism toward the world around you. Being pragmatic is a positive trait, however excessive pragmatism destroys the ability to seize opportunities.

To learn more about the art of embracing opportunities, it is recommended that you continue to work through this book as there is hope for you.

5–8 Points – Your view of life keeps you in the hold of stereotypes and prejudices. This prevents you from benefiting from all the opportunities that are available to you. This is sad because as you miss opportunities, you are missing out on life. In order to rebalance your life, you must start to take bold action. Feel the fear and do it anyway.

9–12 Points – Well done but there is room for improvement! You have the attitude that helps you to identify most opportunities and you are flexible, but you need to develop the strength of conviction and step out boldly to achieve your dreams. Problems and difficulties sometimes scare you. You must work on the weaknesses that prevent you from maximising the opportunities around you. Don't despair, continue to develop with this book and you will learn how to turn those opportunities into tangible values to achieve your goals.

13–16 Points – You are the master of your domain when in the world of opportunities. You are able to seek, identify and seize opportunities to work for you in pursuit of your dreams. You are focused and have an awesome grip on life. Since you already possess a healthy attitude towards life, keep it up and take the challenge of mentoring someone else to help develop themselves and create a value-chain of successes.

Practical Assignments

1. What is your understanding of this phrase: "The man who failed and lost opportunities, wastes his life in vain"?

2. Why is every problem an opportunity? Justify your answer.

3. You have learned not to lose opportunities if they do not fit into your stereotypes and beliefs. List the attitudes and beliefs that prevent you from taking advantage of opportunities.

4. What lessons have you learned on the value of flexibility? Do you consider yourself to be a flexible person? How do you demonstrate flexibility when facing challenges? Give detailed examples.

5. What would you do if you had to work in a way that is not familiar to you? Would you abandon the project?

"Wherever there is an opportunity, there is always an inherent danger or risk". What does that phrase mean to you? What will you do with this knowledge?

Chapter 9

WHY IT IS UNACCEPTABLE TO REFUSE OPPORTUNITIES WHEN THEY ARE OFFERED

Chapter 9
WHY IT IS UNACCEPTABLE TO REFUSE OPPORTUNITIES WHEN THEY ARE OFFERED

In the previous chapter we discussed that when we miss an opportunity, we not only miss that opportunity, but miss out on life in abundance. We examined seven principles, each of which revealing beliefs and behaviours working against us to miss and lose opportunities. In addition to earlier lessons, here are principles revealing the depth of the deception preventing us from realising possibilities:

• It is impossible to identify opportunities. In other words, "There is nothing new under the sun" – Ecclesiastes 1:9. Although this is a biblical truth, it has been wrongly interpreted by many of us so that we are reluctant or even incapable of venturing into the unknown.

• Opportunities do not exist in this environment – nothing new happens here.

- This opportunity is not for me.

- What is the point? I never get recognition for what I do.

- I don't have the resources to execute my goals.

- People do not understand me.

- Opportunities will bring conflicts and contradictions.

- Others may be resistant to my idea.

- What if it does not work?

Never Reject an Opportunity because It Seems Impossible to Achieve

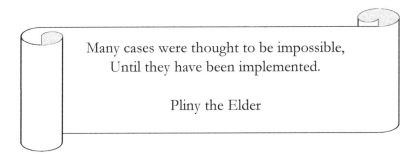

Many cases were thought to be impossible,
Until they have been implemented.

Pliny the Elder

What if it seems impossible? It is always impossible until it is done. All that we enjoy and take for granted now was once in obscurity until someone decided to bring it to life. Planes, cars, the ability to go into outer space, smart phones, cameras, televisions, radios, the internet and email, to name but a few. Even the pens that we write with were once perceived as impossible; in ancient times no one wrote with pen. Some people think that to become a millionaire within 20 years or that a Russia or Ukraine without corruption is impossible. But someone can do it. "Successful things are impossible tasks," said Jacques-Yves Cousteau, the famous French explorer.

How do you make the impossible possible? These are simple practical steps you must take to start:

- Believe in yourself and your abilities.

- Have a strong desire to achieve your goals – all that is possible comes from hard work, so be prepared to sacrifice your time in order to achieve the desired outcome.

- Be persistent, do not give up. You are stronger than you know.

- Be proactive and positive, you will generate the strength needed for the journey.

Let's go back to the story of Thomas Edison, who was also known as "The Magician of Menlo Park". He learnt one paradoxical truth, that **to invent something really incredible, sometimes it is better not to know experts who consider it impossible.** He used a very interesting approach to select his employees. He first introduced the practice of detailed questionnaires. An example of one of his questions would be "who is Plutarch and where is the Volga?" Edison believed inventors are primarily useful for their broad-mindedness and unbiased thinking, and if he had to choose between a "narrow minded specialist" and an "open-minded amateur", often he would choose the latter – a creative genius with no formal education, and in some areas ignorant.

Never Reject an Opportunity because it is New to You

People respond differently to the newness of changes. Some celebrate change, while others are afraid of change. The misconception of familiarity is the enemy of progress and we must do our very best to accept change as a component of opportunity. When a person is averse to change, the consequence is stagnation. Openness to the new is the ability to embrace change with zeal.

How do you become More Open to the New in Your Life?

As long as you keep doing what you're doing, nothing will change. "Doing the same thing over and over again and expecting different results is the definition of insanity," said Albert Einstein, the German-born theoretical physicist, who developed the general theory of relativity. If you want to have something you've never had, start doing something you've never done.

If you want opportunities in your life, you must go beyond your comfort zone, start pushing the boundaries of your reality and stop doubting yourself. Only then will you discover new opportunities that will propel you to greater heights. When confronted with something new, which represents a potential for possibility, your immediate response should be to find courage, the courage to say yes, I can do this. It is necessary to seek understanding so that you can apply the knowledge and skills needed in this new endeavour. Perhaps you can develop by learning through self-education or even formal education, embracing the adventure of the new. You could also network with other people of the same or similar interests. Share your world with like-minded people and people who can help you to the next level.

Never Reject Opportunity because it is of no Benefit to You

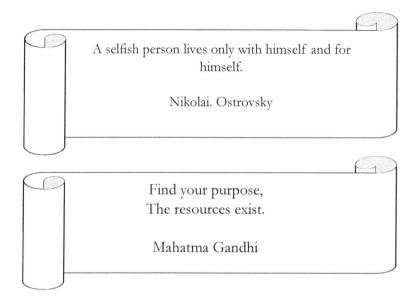

A selfish person lives only with himself and for himself.

Nikolai. Ostrovsky

Find your purpose,
The resources exist.

Mahatma Gandhi

Oksana was doing well in university and her specialty was in languages. One day she received a call for an opportunity with the chamber of commerce. She was required to put her knowledge of the chamber into use with a group from Poland who needed a translator. This was a voluntary job, for which there wouldn't be any remuneration. Although as a student she needed a paid job to help with expenses, Oksana pondered on the offer and eventually decided to accept it.

Two years later, Oksana received an unexpected call from an old acquaintance. One of the Polish visitors had not forgotten the charming interpreter; she remembered how pleasant she had been with them. This visitor had been so impressed by how well Oksana had treated them that she had decided to get in contact to reward her. Oksana was surprised by how generously she was rewarded two years after. Oksana had made the right decision when responding to the initial request to volunteer; her willingness to serve with her talent without any benefit to her at the time paid off two years later.

Despite the inconvenience, Oksana found value in helping others. Although it came years later, fate rewarded her handsomely for her polite and generous heart. The opportunity was presented to her, and she could have said no, since she would have been doing a job without getting paid, but she seized the opportunity. What are the lessons of the story of Oksana? First, the opportunity came to her because she was prepared, and her training in languages put her in a good position to be offered the role. Second, she made a decision by taking the offer. Her selflessness was not in vain.

Often we neglect the opportunities that come our way by our negative self-talk. I do not need this, this is not for me, and I am not wasting my time on this. Even if it does not apply to your field of interest, it came your way for a reason, so why not explore? You never know

–doors could open through this experience in the area of your interest. When a person's reasoning is to focus only on himself, he will inevitably be missing out on the essence of life and as a result on opportunities. This is evident in people who are self-centred; the reward is destruction. "Every man must decide whether he will walk in the light of creative altruism or in the darkness of destructive selfishness," said Martin Luther King Jr., American Baptist minister and activist who was a leader in the African-American Civil Rights Movement. A clear sign of the manifestation of selfishness is focusing only on what involves your agenda and benefits you only. As a remedy, remember this universal principle: what you do selflessly to benefit others returns to you multiple folds. Start doing to others the things you want to experience in your life.

Cultivate the habit of seeking opportunities therefore, especially if they are not of immediate benefit to you, and find those to whom they can be useful, so that you are a solution to the needs of others. It is important to understand that every opportunity is there to meet a need. It is your responsibility to identify those who will benefit from the outcome of the opportunity. "The best way to find yourself, is to lose yourself in service to others," said Mohandas Mahatma Gandhi, the civil rights leader of the Indian independence movement in British-ruled India.

Never Reject an Opportunity for Lack of Resources

The opinion of others about our life is usually
Valued by the weakness of human nature,
Prohibitively high, although the slightest reflection
Shows that this view in itself is
Immaterial for our happiness.

Arthur Schopenhauer

Lack of resources is a common excuse which prevents many people from seizing opportunities that will eventually lead to fulfilment. The typical one is money. "I have no money, no ties, no friend to assist me, no resources" – have you made any of these excuses at some point in your life?

Your belief that you do not have the resources is not an excuse to lose an opportunity. Your inability to identify resources does not mean that the resources are not available. You must follow the steps to review what you have in your hand; the resources you already have could be used in exchange for what you need. Goals are always greater than the resources, so it is your responsibility to use what you have in order to obtain what you need. We are already equipped to be a solution; our job is to put the components together. Like a picture puzzle, you just need to be able to identify the finished product in order to deliver. "Being wise is more important than having money or material goods; wisdom is able to give you all," says Randy Gage. With wisdom you can create value to support your goal of success.

As God creates, He also provides all that you need. However, you must discover and develop His provision in order to convert His creation into reality. Discovering these resources requires time and effort. In your time of discovery, you must remember that everything you have is a resource to be propagated in this life. Everything that God has given you must be used to cultivate – everything including your experience, the way you look and the way you talk, is a tool to achieve a purpose. Most people do not consider their appearance a resource, but this is one of your key resources. Your eyes are a resource, your hair, your voice – every part of you is a resource. The quicker you accept yourself as a resource the quicker you will succeed.

Never Reject an Opportunity because of the Opinion of Others

People often worry that their wife, husband, relatives, neighbours and colleagues don't understand them. As humans, we give the opinions of others more power than necessary. Sometimes it is necessary to pay attention to the opinions of others, however the opinions of others must not be elevated that they take away the desire to do what you need to do. The buck must stop with you. That part of our consciousness which is afraid of condemnation often prevents us from doing things we should do. However, we must be careful to allow this same consciousness to prevent us from our greatest mistakes. The balance must be struck as if the opinions of others do not matter at all, we could, for example, run naked through the street. You have to agree that sometimes the protective function of our consciousness can be useful.

However, the protective function can take on an exaggerated form when the opinions of others begin to control our lives, ideas and opinions. This is wrong. The fear of what people think about us should not prevent us from opportunities. We must not allow other people's opinions to govern our lives.

Others will always have an opinion about you. There are social pressures; we all loath to conform, but for one reason or another we conform. If you take the opinions of others too seriously, your life will not function purposefully, you will be subject to control and in the process lose your freedom and vision. Is your life worth sacrificing for the opinions of other people?

Never Reject an Opportunity because it might bring along Conflicts and Opposition

Julie and Thomas are husband and wife and also partners in business. Their personal relationship experience has not always been positive. In their attempts to make things right in their marriage they tried a number of options, and one of those options turned into a golden opportunity.

One day Julie arrived home from a presentation and with a heavy heart pondered over how she could share her new ideas with her husband. Indeed, their experience of recent business ventures had been one of frustration. They had both agreed never to consider such business deals again. Now she wanted to tell her husband but was worried it would cause another argument. Eventually she took a deep breath and summed up the courage to share her ideas. A few hours later, the couple sat in the kitchen, discussing their plans for the business venture. By the time they were in the middle of discussing the idea, Julie had forgotten the fears that almost prevented her from sharing the great opportunity.

Six months into the business they began to see results. "If not for the courage of Julie...," Thomas thought, smiling at the evening sunset from the window of their cosy kitchen.

The couple's dream came true – they finally achieved the business partnership they had hoped for. Avoiding conflict rather than facing an issue can be a hindrance to great opportunities. You will benefit by heeding the words of Mahatma Gandhi: "First they will not notice you, then they will laugh at you, then they will fight you. And then you will win." Gandhi very subtly describes the process of change. It will be challenging but worth it in the end.

Never Reject an Opportunity because You Could Face Hardship

There is no progress without resistance and restraint. Whenever there is resistance, it is a sign of movement and a product of change. Therefore, resistance, difficulties, disadvantages and obstacles are all signs of progress. Our natural reaction to resistance is doubt; it is normal to doubt from time to time, but the important thing is not to remain in doubt. Do not allow doubt to settle in your heart. The difficulties you encounter along the way are compliments – they are signs you are doing something with your life.

Napoleon Hill, an American author and impresario, devoted his time to studying 22 biographies of successful people in order to unravel the secrets of their success. He found each one of these people quickly discovered and concluded that in every obstacle or trouble, equal in size or more is the opportunity. The lesson here is to embrace difficulties, take the challenge, and develop yourself into a better and smarter being.

Never Reject an Opportunity because of the Fear of Failure

You must not neglect opportunities because of uncertainty or fear of failure. The "what ifs?" that stop us in our tracks may never be realised.

You say "what if it doesn't work, what if I fail?" Chances are it does work, so the question you should be asking is what will I do next once I do succeed? There is only one way to find out. Just do it! Feel the fear and do it anyway.

In search of a better life, Marina came from the provinces of Ukraine to Moscow. She was beckoned by career prospects and higher earnings. Besides, she wanted experience living in a new environment. "Moscow does not believe in tears," as the saying goes. Marina had heard this since childhood, so she came prepared with a brave heart. The capital of Russia won her heart enormously, the fast pace of living intoxicating her.

Life made her truly tempting offers, and though she was not a citizen of Russia, a law firm was ready to take her on with just a diploma and a little experience. As she thought of the opportunities in front of her, fear crept into her mind: "I don't know the Russian law, how will I fulfil my duties?" This was the beginning of the end of Marina's Moscow dream. The rush to conquer Moscow had disappeared, and the strong ambitions were wrapped up silently and buried.

Marina allowed fear to steal the possibilities that could have radically changed her life. In order to prevent fear from stealing your chances in life, you need to learn how to counteract it by setting your mind on the goal.

Fear is always associated with ignorance and uncertainty. If you are afraid, the first antidote is to face the fear and do what you are afraid to do. Success awaits you as you defeat it. You need to calculate all the risks and do everything possible to mitigate them. This is especially relevant in cases when the reason for the fear is a lack of knowledge or understanding. Here you seek the knowledge and understanding you need to eliminate fear.

Alex started a new business just four months ago. The prospects were great with the business promising considerable profit as it was in a rapidly growing sector of online marketing. He had put in a lot of capital to get the business going. As the days went by, the customers were few and far between. Alex was arrested with fear. "How could I have made such a grievous mistake? What if I have invested in something that will not work? Maybe I don't have what it takes to be successful in this business." All sorts of negative thoughts gripped his mind. Realising he needed to do something and do it fast before all hope was lost, he decided to enrol on a course about "How to sell on the Internet". He invested time updating his website, enlisting the help of professionals. Everything went well as his actions paid off. The fear dissipated and his business began to generate a steady income.

Overcoming our fear strengthens us and enhances our ability to take on new opportunities and succeed. Victory over fear is the reassurance that we can do anything if we believe in ourselves. In the words of Russian writer Maxim Gorky, "Weak people expect opportunities and strong people create their strengths". In this chapter we looked at eight reasons we must never decline opportunities:

1. Never pass up an opportunity just because it may be difficult to implement. If an opportunity exists, the tool to see it to fruition is waiting to be discovered.

2. Do not pass up an opportunity because it has never been done before; challenge yourself to greatness. It always starts with one person, let greatness start with you.

3. Never ignore or decline an opportunity because the outcome will not benefit you – do it for the benefit of the people.

4. Lack of resources is not a valid reason to pass up an opportunity.

5. Other people's understanding of the opportunity that comes to you is none of your business. Run your own race.

6. Conflict or contradiction must not stop you from seizing an opportunity.

7. Resistances and challenges are common in opportunities. Don't allow them to stop you.

8. Fear of failure must not defeat you in taking up an opportunity; feel the fear and do it anyway.

Golden Nuggets

Here are the golden truths from this chapter:

1. If you want to have something you've never had, start doing things you have never done.

2. The fewer resources we have at our disposal, the more sensibly we will use what is in our hands.

3. Success is about quality, not quantity. The resources we need are already within our reach.

4. Utilise what you have to attain what you want.

5. We cannot let other people's opinions govern our lives.

6. Even the dead are criticised! Use criticism to your advantage.

7. Progress without resistance is stagnation.

8. The greater the obstacle, the greater the opportunity; obstacles contain troubles equal in magnitude, or even greater than the opportunities.

9. Fear is always associated with ignorance and uncertainty. Do what you need to do to eliminate fear.

This test will help you identify your area of development from this chapter.

Self-Examination Test

1. You just had an argument with a friend. Are you able to continue working with them?

a. No, it will totally throw me off – 0 points;

b. It is very painful for me, and I will survive, but it will affect the quality of my work – 1 point;

c. Yes, although it will not be easy, it should not affect our work – 3 points;

d. Yes, of course! My focus is on the task – 4 points.

2. Do the views of other people strongly affect you?

a. I place a lot of value on what people say about me – 0 points;

b. I conduct myself well, so everyone will be happy with me – 1 point;

c. I would not want people to think badly of me and talk behind my back. It is unpleasant – 2 points;

d. I am completely free from the fear of public opinion – 4 points.

3. Do you think other people's lives are easier than yours?

a. That is exactly the case – 0 points;

b. Yes, it seems that way – 1 point;

c. I don't think so – 2 points;

d. No – 4 points.

4. Have you ever had conflict with anyone in authority, i.e., your teacher, your boss, the government?

a. That would lead to even more problems – 0 points;

b. No – 1 point;

c. In the past, and it was settled – 2 points.

d. Of course yes – 4 points

5. How often do you use these words in your conversations: "It is impossible," "It's unreal," "It never works for me"?

a. My language is composed of these words – 0 points;

b. Quite often – 1 point;

c. Sometimes it slips into my language – 3 points;

d. I don't use such statements; they are of no use. I believe anything is possible if you apply the right attitude – 4 points.

Test Results

Up to 5 Points – You often miss opportunities in your life because you are afraid to venture into the new.

You are happy in your comfort zone and therefore preventing your own growth. Your pessimism is affecting your relationship with those around you. It is not too late to take charge of your life to achieve success. Start by embracing change and take a conscious decision to see the best in every situation. This book will help you identify areas you need to focus on in order to develop the right mind-set for success.

6–10 Points – The fear of the unknown has gripped your heart to the extent that you fail to identify the opportunity in anything that is not familiar to you. The success of others puts you in the state of self-pity which could lead to jealousy and conflict with yourself and others around you. Reading this book has put you on the right path, but you need to take the practical assessments to further understand the areas in which you can focus your development.

11–14 Points – You must develop confidence in yourself. You understand there are opportunities all around you, yet you are falling behind in seizing those opportunities to your advantage. Only you can free yourself from fear; feel the fear and do it anyway. Be consistent in your seeking of opportunities, intensify your efforts and never give up. With time identifying and seizing opportunities will become second nature to you. Continue to read this book, as it will help you improve your skills of converting opportunities into actions and goals.

15–20 Points – you have mastered your best self, and you know and apply the principle of change to your advantage. Your self-belief and ability to identify opportunities is worth emulating. Reading this book is testament to your pursuit of continuing to improve yourself and get the best out of life. Well done. As you know, there is always room for improvement, so use your healthy attitude towards life to encourage others, share your knowledge and create a value chain of success.

Practical Assignments

1. Write down the things you want to do, including things you have never attempted because you thought they were impossible. Now start each item on the list with these words: "How can I do this?"

2. How do you respond to opportunities if you will not be recognised or if the benefit is for others?

3. Why do you believe a lack of resources is a reason to neglect any idea or opportunity?

4. Review the degree of influence of other people's opinions on your life. What do you need to change in this area?

5. Do you refuse opportunities because of conflict with others? How do you plan to improve your skills on resolving conflicts?

6. What are the fears hindering you from seizing opportunities?

7. How do you feel about change?

Following these practical recommendations to cultivate change, start by changing at least one habitual action. In your normal routine for example, if you always go to a particular store or supermarket try another; change your route to work and break a habit. Be conscious of your thoughts and actions.

Chapter 10
WHO RECEIVES
OPPORTUNITIES?

Chapter 10
WHO RECEIVES OPPORTUNITIES?

It took less than a year for an unknown young rapper, Artem Loic, a 4th year engineering student at Poltava National Technical University, Ukraine, to begin to share the stage with famous Russian artists such as Timothy and Gregory Leps. It started from the "New Wave 2013" concert where his popularity among both teenagers and young adults alike was undeniable.

Artem, whose dream is to become a famous rapper, entered the competitions on popular talent shows like "Ukraine's Got Talent"; he had previously been a contestant on the "X Factor" but did not make it as a finalist. Artem did not allow the disappointment of previous competition failures to stop him from achieving his dream. He got on to the third season of "Ukraine's Got Talent", where he show-cased his unique rapping style to the nation. As a finalist on the show, his performance received a standing ovation from both the judges and the audience, the judges unanimously crowning Artem the winner of "Ukraine's Got Talent".

He became an overnight sensation. His unique rapping style and talent meant he was sought after by prominent producers near and far. Gregory Leps, a successful producer, contacted the show's director to meet with Artem. Two days later he was offered a lucrative record deal and signed to Gregory's label.

His advice to Artem was to "work hard" and he will enjoy success. Artem did exactly that and released his first album within a month. As he worked on his second album, he performed free across the country and when asked about this, he responded as follows: "for me this is my big dream, money is secondary. If I think about money, I will not achieve my dreams". Artem continues to develop as an outstanding young man, an influencer on the social scene and in the music industry.

In the previous chapter we examined various reasons why opportunities must be cherished and nurtured in order to achieve success. Now let's examine the question of "to whom do opportunities gravitate?" We will look in detail the seven qualities that you must have so that opportunities will not elude you. The story of Artem exemplifies these principles, as the quality of his skills and his willingness to seek opportunities propelled him to success.

Do What Inspires You

And most importantly, do not worry, feel free to go,
Where your heart and intuition tells you to go.
Somehow they know who you want to actually be.
And everything else is secondary.

Steve Jobs

There is no man living who isn't capable of doing
more than he thinks he can do.

Henry Ford.

Life is full of opportunities through which you can become what you want. A key factor to getting the best out of life is to know your calling. What exactly is a calling? According to the *Dictionary of Psychology*, a calling determines a vocation as a "personal sense of life, transformed into practical purpose". Your calling is part of your uniqueness in this world, a heightened sense of responsibility and value in who you are. My good friend Myles Monroe, consultant and author of bestsellers on leadership, personal growth and spiritual development, defines purpose as follows: it is "the original plan and reason for the existence of a subject, the ultimate goal of existence of the subject". For example, a child whose ambition is to become a musician is told that being a musician is not lucrative and a waste of his time, that he would be better off studying to become a doctor, lawyer, engineer or accountant. As an adult, all grown up and a prominent lawyer who heeded that advice, although his life seems fine, with a respected job and good earnings, he is not satisfied. Why is someone at the top of his profession unfulfilled you ask? The reason for his dissatisfaction is that there is no internal implementation of his ultimate goal of existence. By his nature his desire is music; training and working as a lawyer means he has gone against his nature and is therefore bound to be dissatisfied with life.

Everyone comes into this world with a purpose. Without it, life is aimless, resulting in frustration and disappointment. In the absence of purpose, time loses its meaning, and any effort is a waste of energy. It is impossible to learn how to fully maximise our innate talents. "It does not matter how fast you move if it is not the right destination," said Steven Covey, an American educator, author, businessman and keynote speaker.

Co-founder of the popular social network Facebook, Mark Zuckerberg invested his time in creating a platform to give people the opportunity to share photos and life experiences with their friends and family all around the world. His primary objective was not the money or popularity he would gain from his product. He created a valuable tool, truly loved by the masses worldwide. According to Mark, he was not even going to create a company – he just did what he wanted to see in the world. Remember: "Be the change that you wish to see in the world", said Mahatma Gandhi. "Facebook for me is neither work nor pleasure, it is my mission, which gives me energy, it's the only thing I can do with my life," said Zuckerberg. At the time of his 29th birthday he had created the largest social network in the world and was one of the youngest billionaires on the planet. Mark's experience is an example of opportunity gravitating to a person as he is continually developing new ways to develop his platform. His goal is to create a product that will be a solution; as a product to bring pleasure to the masses, opportunity was inevitable.

It has been scientifically proven that people achieve greater results in an area of interest and passion to them. Unlimited achievements can only be realised if you respond to your calling. Opportunities will gravitate towards you if you are engaged in activities with passion. Hobbies are a good way to deal with stress, and some have taken up a hobby which leads to their vocation. A hobby is described as "a human activity regularly engaged in at leisure for the soul". The main purpose of a hobby is to stir you into fulfilling your potential. Some hobbies have been developed into successful businesses. Ideally you need to engage in activities which stir up a passion in you. You can make money from it if you do it exceptionally well. Self-realisation, the fulfilment of one's own potential, is usually connected to what you do in the majority of your time. Examine yourself, and discover a life of opportunities and fulfilment.

Opportunities gravitate towards those who seek to fulfil their potential by engaging in their calling. Disregard social stereotypes and seize the opportunity from the passion innate in you. What others think of you and what you do is none of their business; do what ignites you and be fulfilled. Find a cause that you love and opportunities will gravitate towards you.

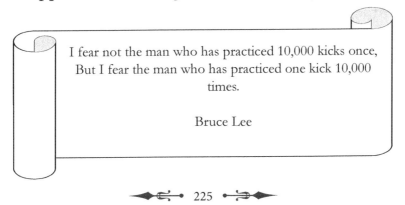

I fear not the man who has practiced 10,000 kicks once,
But I fear the man who has practiced one kick 10,000
times.

Bruce Lee

Now that you know your innate abilities are your best option for a satisfying life, let us go a step further and discover how to stand out so that opportunities gravitate towards you. "Whatever your hand finds to do, do it with all diligence...," Ecclesiastes 9:10. It could be in any area of work as another principle of success is to thoroughly invest your time in what you choose to do. Consistently develop your skills until you are the best at what you do. You will stand out if you are good at what you do; if you are the best you will be unstoppable. Other than you making yourself known, the rest is settled – people will look for your product or service. "Do you see a man skilled in his work? He will stand before kings; he will not stand before obscure men," – Proverbs. 22:29. The co-founder of Facebook developed a product from doing what he loved with the commitment to be the best; today his platform is famous around the world with billions of users.

Once you learn to do something well, continue to practice and develop your craft and opportunities will eventually gravitate towards you. You could start by engaging in your hobby or passion, and do it well. Commitment and focus will also help you on the path to success. "For whatever you decide to do, be the best in the business," said Genichi Kawakami, president of Yamaha motor company, whose motorcycles, along with all their creativity and spirit of competition, became leaders on the world racing stage.

The best way to give yourself a better chance with success is to develop your skills so well that you cannot be ignored. Then and only then will opportunity come and find you.

The Law of 10,000 Hours

What type of people achieve outstanding results? Are outstanding results a coincidence?

In his book *Geniuses and Outsiders*, Malcolm Gladwell, a Canadian journalist and popular sociologist, wrote "what we call talent is the result of a complex web of skills, opportunities and advantages obtained by chance." Twenty years ago, the psychologist Anders Ericsson, together with two colleagues, conducted a study at the Academy of Music in Berlin. Violin students were divided into three groups. The first one included star soloists of world class potential. The second group were rated as promising. The third group were students who had shown an interest in violin and at best taught beginners how to play the instrument. All participants were asked one question, how many hours have you practised from the moment you first picked up the violin?

Although the responses to this question varied, the conclusion was that almost all the students started practising the violin at an early age, at five years old. In the first few years they were engaged for about two to three hours per week. At age eight the differences began to show. The best students practised more than the others, for nine years, approximately – six to nine hours a week – and as they got older they spent several hours training. The highly skilled students invested over 30 hours a week for over 20 years, perfecting their skill. Starting from the age of five, for 20 years the top students invested a minimum of 10,000 hours of training. The middle group invested an average of 8,000 hours, while the future music tutor group invested roughly 4,000 hours of training.

The key observation from Ericcson's investigation is the correlation between time invested and excellence. It is rare to find a single person who has achieved a high level in a skill without consistently investing their time in it over several years. The evidence shows that anyone willing to put the hours of hard-work in will certainly reap the rewards.

Neuroscientist and musician Daniel Levitin writes, "Among numerous studies the following picture emerges in any field: to achieve the level of skill connecting with the status of a world class expert, requires 10,000 hours of practice. Take anyone – composers, basketball players, writers, golfers, pianists, chess players, even inveterate criminals, this number occurs with surprising regularity. Ten thousand hours, approximately three hours of practice a day, or 20 hours a week, for a decade. And yet no one has met the case when the highest level of excellence would be achieved in less time." Besides, the best are not just the students who worked more than all the rest, they worked *much* more. The fact is, achieving mastery in complex activities is impossible without extensive practice – this has been proven time and time again on all professional competences.

Actor Michael Masterson claims that there are four levels to ownership of ability: incompetence, competence, skill and virtuosity. "To overcome incompetence, you need to have practised at least 1,000 hours in your chosen field. To achieve mastery, you need 5,000 hours. Virtuosity is extremely rare, as well as at least 10,000 hours of practice there is evidence of natural talent."

The proven magic number required to achieve mastery is 10,000 hours of groundwork. Question! If you prepare yourself to this level, do you think opportunities will pass you by? Now you know, stop chasing the money. First things first – discover your abilities, invest your time and work to develop yourself. The opportunity you need is guaranteed to gravitate towards you.

Preparation Attracts Opportunities – Be Prepared!

Robin's lifelong dream is to be rich. One day an acquaintance advised him to play the lottery and pray. Robin heeded the advice of praying, he prayed for several days. Suddenly a voice spoke to him: "Robin, how can I answer your prayers to win the lottery, when you have not purchased a lottery ticket?"

This anecdote, though trivial, illustrates the importance of preparation in actualising opportunities. The universe is impartial; God is principled; He is not a magician; anyone who follows His principles will benefit. In order to unleash opportunities, the onus is on you to follow the principles set for the goals to be actualised. The more we are prepared for looming opportunities, the better our chances of success. If we are not preparing to win, it means we are preparing to fail; the one who is not prepared for victory is certainly prepared for defeat.

Preparation attracts opportunities. Lacking in the skills or ability required to implement a task simply means you are not ready for the opportunity. The opportunity will be useless if given to you.

Do you know how an oak tree grows to be so magnificent and useful for so many of the resources we benefit from daily? An oak tree grows very quickly – within a few weeks it can reach an average height of 30 feet. However, before this tremendous growth it could have taken four to seven years from planting to grow out. The growth starts and develops deep down in its root. It develops very strong roots which subsequently explode in the growth seen and used for a variety of products.

The longer and more focused the training, the more you will be eligible for opportunities. People often neglect training, yet demand recognition and success. Many well-known actors and musicians rehearse on the very stage they will be performing on, investing a minimum of three hours of rehearsal daily for months before the concert or show.

Opportunities come to those who are ready physically and mentally for the opportunities that may come their way. Obtain the necessary knowledge and work on your character and put together strategies on your aspirations. "The secret of success is the willingness to use the opportunities when they appear," said Benjamin Disraeli, a former British Prime Minister.

At a minimum you must be educated and competent enough to communicate your ideas and be able to understand at a level equal to the height you want to attain. Unequivocally, a person who has acquired knowledge from a university education adds to his resource in knowledge and will be better prepared to identify opportunities. A higher education qualification is an opportunity in itself; it creates an avenue that may otherwise be closed without the degree.

Preparation time is the period you invest in developing yourself either through formal or informal education.

When a person is not prepared, it predicts defeat. Preparation is the womb of victory to success. A healthy egg and a healthy sperm together have a better chance of producing a healthy baby. Preparation is pivotal to success; it empowers you to be worthy of opportunities to make success a reality.

Motivate Yourself!

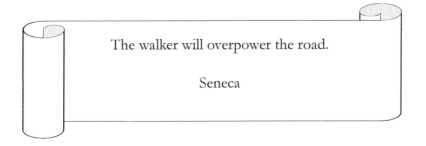

The walker will overpower the road.

Seneca

Two people embarked on a journey in search of their dream. Their path ran between steep mountains and dangerous slopes. Suddenly they stopped at the view of a ledge from a distance. "There is no way ahead! Why do I believe I can make this journey?" the first dream seeker thought to himself. Doubt and fear troubled him until he abandoned his journey and went astray. He believed his eyes instead of his heart and did not continue the journey towards his dream.

The second seeker looked hesitantly at first too. Unlike his companion, he believed he could make the journey, whatever the obstacle. He motivated himself by professing positive words to himself: "I will accomplish my goal, my heart will not deceive me, even if my sight fails." He continued his journey. Approaching the ledge, he was pleased to find the road did not end there, it was just a rock blocking the view from the distance.

The moral of this story is to be determined to follow your cause to the very end. The successful dream seeker teaches us not to be afraid of obstacles, small or big. We must not lose the focus of our journey. Sometimes it is even appropriate to be thankful for the difficulties that help us become stronger.

Opportunity will make way for those who journey towards it. If you stand still, then nothing will change. But if you are constantly moving in the right direction towards your goal, life will eventually reward your efforts with opportunities. Remember the story of the young rapper. If he had sat at home with his talent, maybe his friends and family would commend him if he performed for them and that would be the end of his story. To encounter the opportunity that gave him his big break he had to apply to the show for a chance to showcase his talent. He did not stop there; he also demonstrated his talent by giving an outstanding performance worthy of a standing ovation. Then and only then did the opportunity come rolling in – he became a national sensation, sought after by the industry's best producers.

"A journey of a thousand miles begins with the first step," said Lao-Tzu, an ancient Chinese philosopher and writer. Great things start from humble beginnings. Take the daily steps necessary in the direction of your calling. You don't need to wait for favourable conditions – that is the beginning of laziness and procrastination. "Once your dream is clear to you, you will get the whole world to submit to it. With each day, take a small step closer to your dream," says Randy Gage.

Know and Understand What You Want

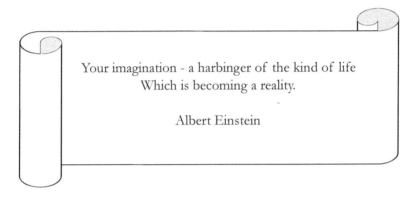

Your imagination - a harbinger of the kind of life
Which is becoming a reality.

Albert Einstein

An artist drew attention from a beggar sitting by the road. Reflecting on wealth that every person inherits, the artist painted this homeless beggar the way he potentially could be. Then he called to the beggar to see his work.

"Is that me?" asked the beggar.

"This is you, as I see you!" said the artist. The beggar was enthused with meaningfulness and new goals.

"If you see me so, then such a person I'll be!" the beggar replied.

The energy we feed our subconscious is the energy that will become our reality. Good or bad, we will receive as ordered. Life will give you what you demand from it. Demand a life of abundance.

A well-planned goal relies on optimism, a strong desire and action. Your beliefs about yourself, your environment and the people around you become your reality. Beliefs and expectations are closely linked. **What you believe is what you get and who you ultimately become.** In other words, you control your own destiny by what you think and what you believe.

You must give energy to the outcome you want to achieve. Your result is determined by your subconscious mind and the information which prevails in the mind will be implemented. If you can conceive it in your mind, you can achieve it. You have the power to eliminate negativity from your life. "Everything is in our hands, so they cannot be lowered," said Coco Chanel, the French fashion designer who founded the fashion house Chanel and had a huge impact on the fashion of the 20th century. Possibilities belong only to those who know what they want from life. "Fortune favours the bold," says the Latin proverb.

Adopt the Right Attitude towards Life

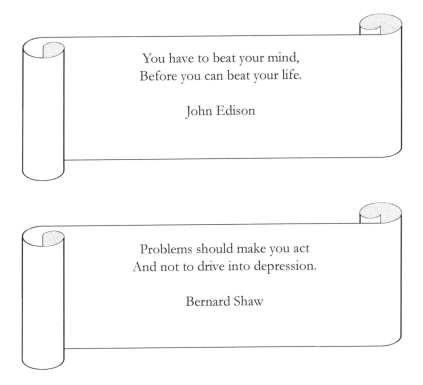

You have to beat your mind,
Before you can beat your life.

John Edison

Problems should make you act
And not to drive into depression.

Bernard Shaw

The notions that circumstances govern our lives and environment shapes our character are the biggest deceptions of all time. It is our beliefs that decide our circumstances. Life is as it is, no matter what happens. What is important is how we react, based on our beliefs. "No one can cause you to feel inferior without your consent," said Eleanor Roosevelt, American social activist and wife of US President Franklin Delano Roosevelt. You determine how others treat you.

Difficult times do not last forever, unless a person determines them to last. "Tough times don't last, tough people do," said Robert H. Schuller, an American pastor, motivational speaker and author. One common view of suicidal people is that they are stuck in a mind-set which dictates life is a one-way street, where everything works and if it doesn't work then life is directed against them. They believe life is controlled by a mystical power and that they have no influence. They see an image that exists only in their head and has no relation to reality. Since they refuse to believe that there are other options, other ways, an alternative to what they see and perceive life becomes unbearable. Refusing to work on and change these false beliefs, they surrender to the mind-set of defeat.

We have a choice in every situation. A person chooses his or her response to any episode in life. The choice to be upset or the choice to rejoice over a matter is entirely up to you. You are in control of your emotions. Don't expect life to be a bed of roses, that you will never make mistakes or that you will always want to choose rejoicing in a situation. However, the power is always in your hands to do as you wish. As humans we also have the ability to determine an appropriate response for a situation; we have in fact mastered this based on our belief system. This explains why we cry when we lose a loved one. An overwhelming feeling of sadness triggers an emotion in us. Even with this trigger, the choice still remains ours. It is certain tough times will come several times in our lifetime and we will make mistakes along the way. However, the important thing to remember is that when you are alive there is hope. "Show me someone who has not made a mistake once in his life, and I'll show you a man who achieved nothing," said Joan Collins, British actress, producer, writer and columnist. No need for self-pity and no apology necessary; turn your mistakes into an experience and knowledge of what not to do next time. The past teaches the present not to repeat the same mistakes in the future. Although life may confront us with problems that seem impossible to resolve, new solutions are never born without errors.

Edison's first patent was in June 1869 for an electronic voting machine. However, the response to the innovation left a lot to be desired, especially amongst politicians on Capitol Hill. After this the young inventor learnt a lesson and a principle which helped him throughout his life as an inventor to "Never invent something that has no demand." Later he would tell reporters "I never feel frustrated because everyone has shown his worthless incorrect attempt, and this is a huge step forward. The only thing that makes me frustrated is when I see how much I can still invent and, at the same time, see how little time I have left."

Positivity combined with simplicity, is one of the key principles to success. Each situation has two sides: you can choose to see it as a complete failure and be consumed with regret, or laugh and learn how to achieve the desired result next time. The ability to admit your mistakes provides you with opportunities for new solutions. There is no need to deny yourself the right to be wrong, otherwise the fear of failure will hold you ransom and deny you the opportunity that can lead to victory.

What do you do if your self-esteem is low? Identify what is causing the low confidence, find out the remedy and work on yourself until you develop your best self-image. The problem many people have with this difficulty is that they become emotionally crippled and surrender to the mediocre, which prevents opportunities from being fulfilled. Whatever makes you feel inferior is a lie, it could be a lie you are telling yourself or a lie from others. The good news is that you can choose not to believe that lie, you can choose to do what you or others believe you cannot do. The power to impart your world is within. Do not underestimate yourself! If you are gifted with an idea it means that there are opportunities to implement that idea. By virtue of the laws of attraction and the subconscious, you will attract into your life everything you need to implement the idea or goal when you believe in yourself and follow the principle required for that goal to be a success.

Free Yourself from Your Inner Barriers

A city zoo keeper was given a polar bear. In order to keep the bear a large cage was needed. The zoo keeper decided to place the bear temporarily in the largest cage available in the zoo, despite it not being big enough for the giant bear. The poor bear paced uncomfortably in the cage all day, taking four steps in one direction then turning around and, after heavily brushing against the cage, taking the other four steps back. After some time, the bear was moved into a new spacious enclosure. However, the bear continued to walk the same old route, four steps to one side then four steps back. In the time the bear was in the small cage, he built another solid cage in his mind: the cage in his mind controlled his actions, even when he was transferred to a bigger space he was still bound by his mind cage. Can you identify with this story? How many times has your mind-set bound you to false beliefs? So often we are like the bear, we limit ourselves and the opportunities given to us. How many cells have you created within yourself? You go only where you allow yourself to go. You want to make a step in the right direction, but the cell you have created sets limits on you, and you stop. This inner cell does not develop without the boundaries created in your mind. Would you agree with me and start freeing yourself from the self-imprisonment of your mind? You may not even be aware of where this has come from or you may be deluded by the self-imposed prison; now that you know, give yourself permission to be free of any limitation. Exercise your freedom today.

Beliefs create motives – the motivation to do what we need to do is developed from our belief system. "Guard your heart with all diligence; for out of it are the issues of life," Proverb 4:23. Whatever you call true is true, your beliefs are those generalisations based on past experiences, but they have no logic, they cannot prove anything. Beliefs for future events or outcomes are working on hypotheses which are yet to be proven. The only person that can prove your hypothesis is you, and you can only prove this hypothesis when you take action. The knowledge that it happens to someone else does not apply to you. Once a different variable (you) is involved, it is a totally new experience and the outcome is open to change. This is not to dispute that something happened to form your belief in the first place; however, that was in the past, once relevant, but now time and chance have taken place and past outcomes do not determine the future and should not control your behaviour. If your consciousness is not burdened with unfortunate beliefs and stereotypes you live a better life.

Winners' vs Losers Mind-set

The winner is always part of the answer,
The loser is always part of the problem.
The winner always has a plan,
The loser always has an excuse.
The winner says, "Let me do that for you",
The loser says, "It's not my job."
The winner sees an answer to every challenge,
The loser sees a problem in every answer.
The winner sees green grass even in the desert,
The loser sees a wasteland on a green meadow.
Winner "It is difficult, but possible!"
Loser "It is possible, but too difficult..."

Anonymous

All of these differences stem from our thoughts. In turn, they are projected onto the way we relate to our world. The more a person is free from internal barriers, the more doors of opportunity will open.

In this chapter we have examined seven qualities we must develop to seize opportunities. Here is a quick recap:

1. Work on what inspires you

2. Become the best at what you do

3. Be prepared

4. Motivate yourself

5. Understand what you want

6. Formulate the right attitude to life

7. Free yourself from inner barriers

Golden Nuggets

1. Life is what you make of it.

2. Be the best you can be, in whatever you do.

3. To achieve the status of an expert, you must practise your skills for 10,000 hours.

4. For an opportunity to win, you must follow the principles. Think of the United Kingdom lottery slogan: "Playing makes it possible". First you select a set of numbers of your choice, then you pay for it to play; finally you check if you have won.

5. Preparation attracts opportunities.

6. Be ready to take chances to acquire opportunity, learn to identify opportunities.

7. Opportunities come to those who make a move towards their goal. A journey of a thousand miles begins with one step.

8. Life will give you what you order. Chose well, chose according to your calling.

9. Difficult times cannot last forever, but if you insist they will.

10. You have a choice in every situation, choose right.

Complete the test below to give you an indication of your understanding of this chapter:

Self-Examination Test

1. I often find myself thinking that I am not in the right job.
a. Yes – 0 points;
b. To a certain extent yes – 1 point;
c. I am satisfied, I will move on when I am ready – 3 points;
d. I am completely satisfied with my business/career – 4 points.

2. Which statement best describes you and the effort you put into your work/business?

a. Horses die because of work – 0 points;

b. Honestly, I do what I need to do to get paid – 1 point;

c. I try to be guided by this principle of hard work, but I believe I could do better. – 3 points;

d. My ethos is to be the best in everything I do, I follow this principle always – 4 points.

3. Do you have a hobby, a favourite pastime that you adore, which gives you lots of joy?

a. What hobbies? Thank God, the children and family are ok. What else do you need in life? – 0 points;

b. No, nothing specifically – 1 point;

c. I am developing my hobby by attending workshops and seminars to improve my knowledge – 2 points;

d. Yes, I have a hobby I am very passionate about – 4 points.

4. The road needs walkers – which of the following statements closely explains this statement in relation to your life?

a. At the present moment I have no strength or motivation to move forward – 0 points;

b. I wish I had the drive – 1 point;

c. I am cheerfully moving forward, though I could be faster – 3 points;

d. Clearly, I'm on the way to my goal – 4 points.

5. Do you have internal barriers?

a. Very much – 0 points;

b. It bothers me how much I do – 1 point;

c. I am constantly working on my internal barriers; I know they are not true – 3 points;

d. At the moment I have reached complete freedom from internal barriers – 4 points.

Test Results

Up to 5 Points – There are opportunities around you, but you rarely notice, let alone make use of them. Most likely you have submitted to the belief that opportunities do not exist for you. This belief maybe due to low self-esteem and the presence of strong internal barriers that hinder your development in this area. Your lack of passion and focus means you have no real ambition to work on. Don't despair, it is not too late to develop the right mind-set to help you identify opportunities. You need to develop a more optimistic attitude to start with. You are in control of your life and not the other way round; life is for you to take dominion. Further reading of this book can help you correct these weaknesses.

6–10 Points – Most opportunities pass you by because you have trouble identifying your calling and developing the right attitude towards life. You are slow to make a move and subsequently lose opportunities; you are bound by self-imposed limitations. You need to develop qualities to help you identify and attract opportunities. Use the practical exercises to get you started.

11–15 Points – You are in good company with this book, you already possess some of the attitude and belief systems to help you identify and seize opportunities. You lack self-confidence and zeal to do the things you really want. Stop giving in to fear, focus on developing yourself and surely you will succeed. Set plans and put them in motion, be relentless in pursuing your goals. Don't take any opportunity for granted, use challenges as a stepping stone to the height of success. Develop using the opportunities to achieve set goals. This book will help you, so use the practical tasks to start a strategy for your development.

16–20 Points – You have a great result! Congratulations! You are in your vocation and confidently moving through life. You have the right attitude towards life, so with such potential you should share your skills with others! Be a mentor and help someone else develop their confidence and ability to identify and make use of opportunities.

Practical Assignments

1. Analyse the life of Artem – the Ukrainian rapper. What character traits and behaviours do you observe from his story? How did his beliefs support his dreams?

Passion is vital in seizing opportunities! Evaluate your passion with the following:

- What do you enjoy doing without being asked?

- Are you willing to devote your life to your passion?

- What profession is aligned with your hobby?

- In what area are you an expert?

- What do you do well? What distinguishes you from the crowd?

Identify your passions and devote yourself entirely to them. Work hard to become the best in your chosen passion. Explore and discover new things. Be a trend-setter don't wait for others to determine the direction of your passion. Observe the lives of successful people, learn from their experience and develop your own success story from your calling.

Once you figure out your true passion, make it a habit and live it every day. For a better understanding of this topic, read the book; *Who am I? How to Find Yourself by Sunday Adelaja.* Write 10 to 20 lessons you learnt from this chapter – what's new to you and how do you plan to implement it?

Select a specific niche and become the best in it. Be determined to immerse yourself in developing and practising skills necessary for you to clock up 10,000 hours. How many hours can you apply daily to reach at least competency level? What strategies will you use to achieve your training goals?

1. **Review your lifestyle: are you moving forward in your goals or standing still? How fast are you moving?** Have you chosen the correct path? Identify and list the steps to help you move your goals forward. How do you plan to engage in a continuous process of achieving your goal?

2. **Opportunities come only to those who are prepared.** Write down the five spheres where you are not yet prepared for opportunities. Go over the practical steps required to be prepared and develop yourself to achieve them.

3. **Rate your self-esteem,** is it preventing you from seeking and seizing opportunities? If this is an

area for improvement, I recommend you read books on freedom from fear, rejection and low self-esteem.

4. Observe yourself: what are the negative stereotypes and beliefs you hold that run contrary to your inner desires, preventing you from reaching your potential? When you think back and realise the effects of your attitudes and beliefs, you will understand why you are so often missing life's opportunities.

Chapter 11

OPPORTUNITIES COME TO THOSE WHO ARE PERSISTENT

Chapter 11
OPPORTUNITIES COME TO THOSE WHO ARE PERSISTENT

In the previous chapter we examined seven qualities necessary to be open to possibilities. In this chapter we are turning our attention to the qualities opportunities favour.

Opportunities come to those who are persistent and persevere

If you really want something, you
Should achieve it on your own and with
The whole purpose. Nobody is going to
Give you this, and if you hesitate or doubt, you will
surely fail.

Chuck Norris

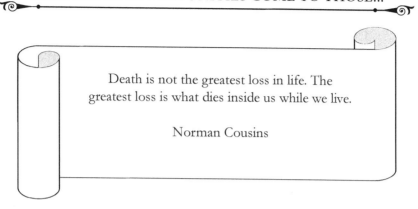

Death is not the greatest loss in life. The greatest loss is what dies inside us while we live.

Norman Cousins

Opportunities come to those who are persistent – they have the tenacity to work on their goal until the end. These people are assertive and take responsibility for their choices. Such people persevere with their education and training and receive great outcomes.

Even when a situation becomes difficult, once the goal is clear the journey will continue until the goal is achieved. Loyalty to your goal is perseverance. It is very easy to drop everything and give up when the going gets tough. "Develop success from failures. Discouragement and failure are two of the surest stepping stones to success," said Dale Carnegie, an American writer and lecturer and developer of famous courses in self-improvement. When you feel sadness and lack of motivation, know that you're almost done. "Never, never, never give up!" said Winston Churchill. Giving up is not an option in the world of opportunity and success.

Let's go back to the story of Thomas Edison. If you recall, he was the world famous American inventor and entrepreneur who perfected the telegraph, telephone and cinematographic equipment, built the first electric voting machine, marked the beginning of electronics and invented the phonograph and one of the first commercially successful electric incandescent options. When he was searching for a suitable material for his incandescent electric lamp he went through about 6,000 samples of materials before settling on bamboo. While examining the features of the coal chain lamp, he invested his time in the laboratory, approximately 45 hours straight without rest. Until very old age, he worked 16–19 hours a day. Nikola Tesla, inventor in the field of electrical and radio engineering, engineer, spoke of his rival: "If Edison had a needle in a haystack, he would not waste time trying to determine its most probable location. Instead, he would immediately, with the feverish diligence of bees, begin to examine straw after straw until he found the needle."

Thomas Edison is the creator of many great inventions: in his lifetime the US Patent Office issued over a thousand patents on his request. No other single person has ever been credited to so many patents. Are all those wonderful opportunities a coincidence or did he give all that he could to achieve greatness? Edison is an outstanding example of a persistent person.

According to him, perseverance is a necessary quality in order to achieve even the slightest success. Although people fail from time to time, that should never stop us in our tracks. Failure should be a stepping stone and a springboard for the next take off. In all failure cases, we owe it to ourselves and life to try again until we achieve our goal or better. If you are willing to give up with every difficulty then, most likely, opportunity is not in good company. "A man who does not tend to fight for what he wants is not worthy of owning what he wants," said Frederic Beigbeder, contemporary French novelist, essayist, literary critic and editor.

"The secret of genius is work, perseverance and common sense," said Thomas Edison. This summarises the answer to the topic of this chapter. Hard work and persistence will automatically provide you with the necessary aptitude for taking advantage of opportunities.

Opportunities Gravitates To Those Who Are Open to Receive

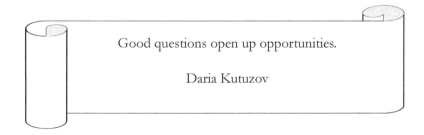

Good questions open up opportunities.

Daria Kutuzov

Christmas mornings are magical, the view through the window is of gently falling snow. The fresh winter air fragrant with the scent of tangerines. A young man walks away from the window, smiling mysteriously. He has hidden his wife's gifts in the living room, hoping to surprise her while she is still asleep. Not long after, she is up and ready for the day. Victor eagerly informs his young wife that Santa Claus was here earlier and has hidden gifts for her. With a spirited smile Angelina begins searching for the hidden surprises. With zeal, it takes her no time to discover three gifts. She thanks her husband with joy as she settles to unwrap her gifts. "There are more," the young man announces. Angelina immediately sets for further searches. She manages to find a couple more gifts, then both with pleasure sit down for breakfast.

As they tuck into their food, Victor comments: "It's a shame you have not discovered the best gifts yet." At the same time his eyes begin to sparkle. "What else is there darling?" Angelina asks incredulously. "There are ten gifts," Victor proudly announces. That is enough to make the young woman forget her breakfast and courteously explore every nook and cranny of their home. She looks in places she has searched previously, only this time she is sure additional gifts are hidden and must be found. Angelina eventually finds all ten gifts.

The amusement of the hide and seek was remembered between the couple for years to come. It is important to note these points from the story of Victor and Angelina. If Victor had not said anything, then Angelina would have been content with the three gifts she found on her first attempt at searching. Understanding there are additional opportunities, she continued in her search for the remainder of the gifts. Her ignorance of additional gifts deprived her of vision, not knowing there were more surprises in store for her. The moral of the story is: opportunities can only come to those who see them. What is sight? The faculty or power of seeing is not limited to the eye only – you must dream, imagine, search and seek. In order to engage with opportunities, you must first apply sight to knowledge. When we have no knowledge or understanding, we will be blind to a situation; the only remedy to blindness in this context is knowledge. "My people perish for lack of knowledge," Hosea 4:6. This demonstrates the value of knowledge. Day in, day out, people live their lives ignorant of the opportunities that await them. This type of blindness destroys life, destroys destinies and shatters hopes. The antidote to destruction is to seek knowledge to unveil the opportunities all around you.

You also need to acquire wisdom – the quality of having experience, knowledge and good judgement.

Wisdom also requires the ability to see and seek the qualities of opportunities. Wise people are thinkers, they ask questions and look for solutions. "A wise man sees before him an immeasurable realm of the possible, a fool considers possible only what is," said Denis Diderot, French writer, educator, philosopher and playwright.

The ability to see determines how far you will go in life; for this reason, we must also develop the skills of analysing and developing the ability to listen, perceive and take action.

Opportunities Come to Those Who Ask Questions

Opportunities come to those who ask questions. Questions are the "hook" to knowledge and information, hence the sign (?) is like a hook. Questions are active tools to obtain information and open new opportunities. Intelligent people are always curious and they ask questions until they get the answer to solve the mystery of the problem.

In the 18th century, French politician Gaston de Levis observed that "The human mind is easier to judge by his questions than by his answers." As children we are taught not to ask stupid questions and so many of us as adults still feel restraints to probe in the fear of appearing stupid. When a person asks questions the opportunity to increase in knowledge and understanding is ignited. The bible also encourages us in many ways to "Ask and it will be given to you; seek and you will find; knock and the door will be opened to you," Matthew 7:7. Anyone who does not ask gets no response and denies himself of the opportunity of an answer. The one who asks sends a request to receive a response and receive new knowledge.

Statistics show that the number of successful people in any society is estimated to be around 3% of the world's population. These are the most "ambitious" – those who yearn for at least some progress for themselves and want to change the world. They are intense, relentless and consistently pursue goals and seek out the best in all of their endeavours.

Success vs Failure: Match the type of person to each statement:

- Am I able to?

- What do I want?

- How do I get it?

- That's impossible

- How to do it?

- I cannot do it.

- What do I need to change in order to get it done?

- How will I do it?

I hope you enjoy this elementary-style game. On a serious note, which category of person are you? The type of questions you ask could also determine your success rate. First thing first – it is better to ask questions than none at all and live in oblivion.

Here is another example of using the right type of question to categorise success verses failure. Persons A and B are both paid equal salaries, and they both want to buy a property to have their own home. Person A asks himself the following questions: "What type or size of property can I get with my current income? What do I need to do to get the ball rolling? What additional part-time jobs should I take? What information do I need to achieve this goal? Do I need to increase my income? What type of job can I do with my current skill to increase my salary? Or what type of business can I start to increase my income so that I can achieve the objective of buying a property?" Person B says: "Am I unrealistic to have this desire to buy a property?" "It is not possible with my current salary" "The property business is risky; can I afford to take any risks?" Person B's questions are all negative self-talk. In this scenario, who do you think is likely to succeed? Questioning is vital to understanding and with understanding and corrective action, success is assured.

The very formulation of the questions of both person A and B is interesting. In an observation of American and European attitudes, Americans favour asking questions with a "How?" while Europeans (especially in Russia), usually ask "Why?". These is indicative of why the largest percentage of millionaires, inventors and entrepreneurs are from America. "How" looks to the future, calling to action, and "why" explains and puts an end to the question without seeking a solution. To seize opportunities, you must develop the "How" mentality.

Opportunities Come to Those Who Constantly Work on Themselves

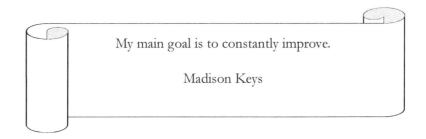

My main goal is to constantly improve.

Madison Keys

Opportunity beckons those who are lifelong learners. These people actively seek to self-educate to always improve their knowledge. In the process of continuous improvement, they critically approach each new situation by paying attention to details and critically analysing their world to provide solutions. "If I take some little thing in my hand, then I immediately begin to think how it could be improved," – Guglielmo Marconi, an Italian inventor and electrical engineer known for his pioneering work on long-distance radio transmission.

It is vital to critically evaluate the outcome of your labour. Only by doing so will you improve and give birth to new ideas.

Here are a few tips from the famous blogger Leo Babauta about how to regularly improve your skills.

1. **Leave time to explore the new.** Perhaps it would be 30 minutes per day or 1 hour a week, either way it is important that you leave time to regularly learn something new in your profession or area of interest. This may be by reading a book, a magazine or a blog on the internet – study the work of successful people. You can even attend formal part-time/evening classes if it suits your learning style. The idea is to broaden your knowledge and develop your skills. Whatever you do, do not miss the time allocated for training weekly.

2. **Think about what you are doing.** Many of us do the same work for so long that we stop thinking about it – that's a bad sign as your work will be of the same level and your skills will not improve. Think about what you are doing and always try to find a way to do your job better.

3. **Work on yourself.** Once you start thinking about what you are doing, you need to pay attention to how you are doing it. Analyse your skills, find out what you did well and what you need to improve. Any workflow, even extreme waste, can be improved.

4. **Seek inspiration.** If you're good enough and consistently doing your job, it can be difficult to find the motivation for further development. In that case, look at the work of others, especially those at the top of their game in your profession or craft. Find the masters and subject matter experts often, this can be enough to understand what it takes to develop and get enough motivation. Try to keep track of the best in your field, and you will always have the motivation for further development.

5. **Learn from the best.** Study the masters in detail, read about them and what they are saying. If possible, learn directly from the master. Cooperate with them, be in their team and work in their company,

perhaps on a joint project. Nothing will teach you better than to work with someone who really knows what to do. Pay attention to everything they do and ask questions. Remember, the master became who they are by learning from former masters.

6. **Look for criticism.** Sometimes it's hard to see your mistakes because you are so immersed in the work. Therefore, a fresh look is always useful. Ask someone you respect to criticise your work, while being very honest. Do not be offended and discouraged by the criticism as all criticism is useful; try to use it to your advantage and improve your craft. Be sure to take note: write down everything that drew the attention of the criticism and look for ways to improve each item.

7. **Attend seminars or courses.** Though you can get the same information from books, audio books, videos and other sources through the Internet, attending classes focuses your attention on the time invested to sit and digest the information. Also, the interaction with the tutor and other classmates has some advantages. It will contribute to a better understanding of the topic material and give you more insight into the understanding of other attendees. You will also have an opportunity to receive feedback from your peers.

8. **If the work is boring, it's time to work on your goals.** If you are bored working, then most likely

you are no longer setting new goals for yourself. Sometimes there is no need to change the profession as a simple look at what you do could make all the changes. Give yourself a worthy objective, raise the bar. American author and Pastor William Arthur Ward held the following recipe for success: "Study while others are sleeping; work while others are loafing; prepare while others are playing; and dream while others are wishing." Live according to this recipe and you are sure to encounter opportunities that lead you to success.

Opportunities Come to Those Who Go the Extra Mile

Another sure way of encountering opportunities is in the willingness to do what is required, with consistent effort and doing more than is expected of you. For example, if you are learning a foreign language and you are set to learn five new words a day, double your efforts by studying and memorising 10 words. If you are expected at a business meeting for 9am be there by 8.30am. If you have the opportunity to improve yourself by additional training from your employer, take the time to engage with your learning and development department to start your learning immediately; be enthusiastic and work hard.

Go the extra mile every day of your life. Few expect more than is asked. By doing a little more than is required of you, you will gain the respect and recognition that will return dividends in the form of opportunities. These are the factors that are often neglected. For example, increase the working day for at least half an hour! You will find that not many people do this, and for that reason you may ask, "If there's no one doing this, why should I?" That is why the "extra mile" is such a lonely place, but by the same token there are so many possibilities there.

How to apply this? Go early, leave late, make an additional call, send an additional letter, devote additional time to market research, help the client to pack and unpack the goods without waiting to be asked. Do not just tell your employees what to do, show them how to do it, and work side-by-side with your subordinates. Whenever you do something, think about what you can do as an additional step, especially if other people are not taking this step.

Charles Kendall Adams, an American educator and historian, once said "Nobody has ever had success by simply doing what was required only. To succeed, you need to do much more." He was later echoed by Andrew Carnegie, an American businessman and philanthropist: "Someone who does not do what he is told will never make it to the top, and neither will the one who does not do more than he is told." People who do less than what it takes deprive themselves of the opportunity to move forward and succeed.

If you are willing to go the extra mile, making the extra effort, doing a lot more than required and work hard, you will have a good chance to grasp the opportunities not open to others who have not invested the same amount of time and effort as you. If you want to have opportunities come to you, you must learn to do more than is obligatory; go above and beyond.

Opportunities Come to Those Who Are Ready to Work on Themselves

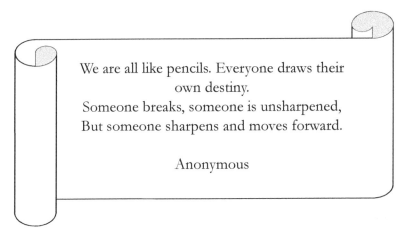

We are all like pencils. Everyone draws their own destiny.
Someone breaks, someone is unsharpened,
But someone sharpens and moves forward.

Anonymous

You must be willing to improve yourself both professionally and personally. If you are to rise from one level to another, you must find the best opportunities at each level. There are principles that govern this; everyone has the potential to grow. To improve your abilities you must improve your skills. As your skills grow you improve yourself and become open for new opportunities.

Personal growth is crucial for career advancement and self-development. The studying of new material helps you to grow and enables a better understanding of life. Working on yourself is never a waste of time, it is an investment that will open new perspectives. A wise man once said, "Yesterday I was clever and wanted to change the world. Today I am wise and so I am changing myself" – Rumi, thirteenth century Persian poet.

How to start working on yourself:

1. **Read daily** – There are treasures hiding in books, they can take you to whole new worlds.

2. **Learn new languages** – Acquiring a new language enables new skills, and invites you to other cultures.

3. **Find a hobby** -Perhaps it will be the old or the new craze in the usual or a completely new interest.

4. **Attend workshops, courses and lectures** – they are great ways to gain new knowledge and skills.

5. Create a positive atmosphere around you – It is always the things around us that affect our mood. Befriend the positively charged and draw a daily source of inspiration.

6. Use your day productively – Wake up early, it will increase productivity and positively affect the quality of your life.

7. Be active – Exercise regularly and maintain a healthy body and mind.

8. Set targets – Achievable targets achieved can be a great source of motivation. Take a little step towards your goal daily.

These simple steps will increase your chances of identifying opportunities in your path.

Opportunities Come to Those Who are aware of their Environment

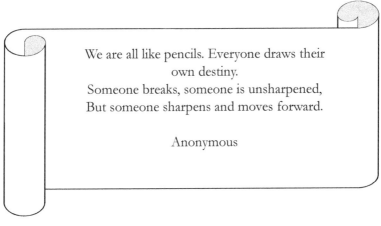

We are all like pencils. Everyone draws their own destiny.
Someone breaks, someone is unsharpened,
But someone sharpens and moves forward.

Anonymous

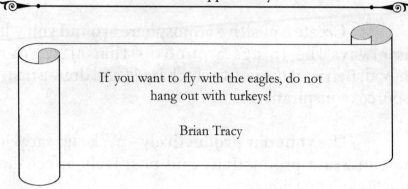

If you want to fly with the eagles, do not
hang out with turkeys!

Brian Tracy

Our environment is not just the location or the area in which we live. Environment can be any form of influence, it can be parents, friends or colleagues. The influence of those we interact with regularly is part of our environment and it can greatly impact on our life, our goals, our intentions and behaviour. A Russian proverb puts this simply: "To live with wolves, howl with them." It means we foster the characters of those with whom we spend our time.

Environmental influences unchecked can be much stronger than factors such as knowledge or character. If you compare the influences that inform your beliefs the chances are the environment will be top of your list. The bible says, "Evil communications corrupt good manners," 1 Cor.15: 33. The company that you keep is vital to your well-being. Humans are born inherently good, but they are shaped by their environment. Even if you are from a good family, who you engage with mostly will influence your character.

You should be able to identify with this by observing your own life. Many people are addicted to smoking and drinking because of the company they kept when they were young or the people that influenced them as youths. Many former drug addicts and alcoholics who have found freedom can testify to this; most will admit they are from very good families and had an excellent education but were caught up with the wrong crowd.

Create Your Environment

What do you want from your life? Figure out your environment and control it to mirror what you want in life. Your environment should match your goals to draw inspiration and to challenge you always to be the best. You need to consciously build, create and seek that environment, which will help you to achieve your goals. Choose your friends carefully, make sure your friendships and goals are aligned. Strengthen your character, gain inspiration from positive-minded people. You must consciously create your surroundings!

Being outside the environment of their vocation, a person automatically loses 50% of their potential success rate. Do your upmost to be in your area of calling: life will make more sense in the environment of your vocation. There is a right environment to make you the person you want to become. Find that environment, as ignoring this principle is as absurd as the dream of becoming a musician but never showing any interest in music, or not being able to sing at all. The environment is vital in creating the prerequisites of success!

Formal education should be a minimum precondition, no matter what your ambition. If a person wants to become a lawyer, a politician or a president, of course he needs to go to school and get an education, but this is not enough. In addition to theoretical skills and knowledge in the area of your chosen profession, character and the right environment are pivotal to success. Let's take politics as an example. If you have not joined a party and made yourself known by becoming an active member of the party, your knowledge and understanding of politics will not be enough to get elected. Being in the right environment and having the right character for the part also matters.

We all know people in positions of authority. Take politicians for example, all of them are ordinary men and women like us. However, in order to attain office, they had to make themselves known. What allowed them to take position in the highest legislative body of the country is not just about having the knowledge, but also putting their beliefs into action in the right environment – the environment where they engaged to showcase their knowledge. The point is of course there are people more qualified and knowledgeable than some of the politicians we know, but if they are not engaging in the right environment we will never know them and they will never attain office. The fact is, it does not matter, and the position can only be occupied by being in the environment and making your work known. Often, those who are more moral with intellectual qualities quietly sit at home thinking "it's none of my business, I know nothing", negatively self-talking themselves down. "The only thing necessary for the triumph of evil is for good men to do nothing," said Edmund Burke, an Irish statesman. As we frequently witness in today's society, many atrocities have been committed because those who have the solution have been quiet and in obscurity. Doing something successfully requires the right environment, motive and action.

A Good Environment is an Incubator for New Opportunities; your Network, your Net Worth

Your environment is full of great resources for opportunity. The success of those you engage with will motivate you also to succeed. Be mindful of the company you keep, as your company has a significant influence on your resolve and result. Surround yourself with the right kind of people – those with values and aspirations to reach the optimum level of success. "Your network is your net worth," said Tim Sanders, author, public speaker and former Yahoo director. Real success is achieved with the support and participation of others; the efforts of one is of no comparison to the effort of a team.

It is an undeniable fact that your environment affects you. The decision to change yourself and your life is in your hands, so take the necessary actions for a life of unlimited opportunities.

Opportunities Come to Those Who Have a Commendable Mentor

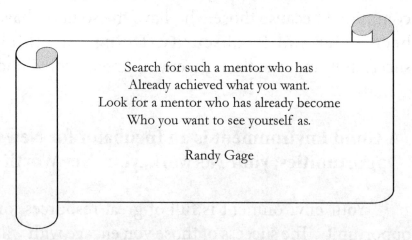

Search for such a mentor who has
Already achieved what you want.
Look for a mentor who has already become
Who you want to see yourself as.

Randy Gage

If you blame others for your failures, do you also pay tribute to others for your success? Behind every successful person are always other successful people.

In this digital age and with the advent of social media we are roped into following and 'liking' people, and there is nothing wrong with this if it is done purposefully. Follow the examples of those who are successful, particularly in your area of calling – emulate the masters. It is always an advantage to have a mentor who can guide and help you find the right direction and who can help develop solutions to issues; someone who has had similar experiences to gain empathy with you and an understanding of your issues. Familiarise yourself with people who have bigger dreams. The difference between the poor and the rich is their "mind-set" – the way they think and overcome obstacles," – Dexter Yager, one of the largest sales professionals in the United States.

Truly successful people always have something to share – they have some experience of what works and what does not. If you manage to find a mentor who will share with you the secrets of success, the outcome of your experience with a mentor will be invaluable. The effectiveness of your efforts will multiply. We must always be learning in order to grow, so why not learn from those who are already at the heights we intend to attain. For example, if you copy the behaviour of an alcoholic it is easy to guess what will happen in that scenario, so using the same formula emulate the actions and deeds of outstanding mentors to give you an edge in any opportunity. Imitating success, multiplies successful. This is the shortest way to the growth of any individual. "Three paths lead to wisdom: first, by reflection, which is noblest; second, by imitation, which is easiest; and third by experience, which is the bitterest," said Confucius, the ancient Chinese thinker and philosopher, whose teachings had a profound impact on the lives of people in China and East Asia. It was the basis of their system of philosophy known as Confucianism.

Another important aspect you should consider when choosing a mentor is you have to seek your mentor. Don't wait for the mentor to come to you, the student must go to the teacher. It should be noted that everyone has come into this world to fulfil their own purpose in life. No one will be able to learn your lessons. Even with the help of a mentor, the onus is on you; the support of a mentor should complement your will and desire for your life. You must be ready for the process of change.

Did you know that some people are fine with their situation, even when it leaves nothing to be desired? It is like being chronically ill but not wanting a cure. Statistics show that only 30% of people who go to doctors follow the doctor's advice. Many do not go to the doctor at all, so they eliminate themselves from obtaining a remedy. Some prefer only to ease the symptoms as a temporary measure. Often between the doctor and patient there is an unwritten agreement: the doctor promises not to doubt the patient, if he pretends to implement all the recommendations of the doctor.

Experience shows that it is of little use when change is imposed. It usually ends in disaster. We must be willing to work on ourselves and access the true benefit of seeking opportunity for our own personal success.

If you are lucky enough be close to a person who is already successful in an area you are seeking, you should cling on to them and learn from their experience. It is also useful to study the biographies of great men and women and make a mentor amongst the prominent figures of our time. You will increase your chances of encounters with the opportunities that you need for the advancement of your goals. You may not always understand the reason behind the advice of your mentor or why it is necessary to go through the direction they advise, but sometimes you have to just decide to be obedient to the cause. For personal coaching and mentorship programmes go to sundayadelajablog.com.

Before we examine the final chapter of the book, "Life is an opportunity", here is a reminder of the key points from this chapter:

- Persevere

- Perceive

- Ask questions

- Constantly improve

- Do more than is required of you

- Be willing to work on yourself and work on yourself

- Create the right environment for your goals to flourish

- Get the right mentor

If you carefully study each of these eight characteristics and begin to apply the knowledge to your life, you will greatly increase the likelihood and speed of bringing new and exciting opportunities your way. Use this list to remind yourself of the main ideas that are contained in this chapter. Here are the golden truths:

Golden Nuggets

1. There are no situations or problems without solutions.

2. The man who is not inclined to fight for what he wants, is not worthy of it.

3. Opportunities meet those who walk towards them.

4. If a person does not ask questions, he deprives himself of the opportunity to get answers.

5. The small becomes large only to those people who critically assess their work.

6. People who do less than what is required deprive themselves of the opportunity to move forward and succeed in life.

7. We are all like pencils. Everyone draws their own destiny. Some are broken, some are unsharpened, and some are sharp and move effectively.

8. Real success is achieved by the support and participation of others and it always includes the input and participation of others.

Take this test to examine the level of your ability in the areas addressed in this chapter.

Self-Examination Test

1. It seems to me that the perseverance in me is greater than my abilities.

a. I strongly disagree with this statement – 0 points;

b. This is partially true – 1 point;

c. I am a very persistent person – 3 point;

d. Persistence is one of my strong qualities. I always continue until I reach my goals – 4 points.

2. My friends have similar or higher levels of ambition than me.

a. No, my friends have less ambition – 0 points;

b. I feel a shortage of such people in my environment – 1 point;

c. Our ambition levels vary; most are similar to me, not higher – 2 points;

d. I'm in an environment of like-minded people of high ambition – 4 points.

3. How often do you question your life?

a. Never, my life is what it is – 0 points;

b. Rarely – 1 point;

c. Quite often – 3 points;

d. Asking questions is part of my personality; it is a necessity for me in order to analyse and evaluate my growth – 4 points.

4. I always do more than is required of me.
a. I don't see the point – 0 points;
b. If I have to – 1 point;
c. For the most part – 3 points;
d. I always go the extra mile; it gives me pleasure – 4 points.

5. I am always working on myself.
a. I have done all the work I need to do – 0 points;
b. If it is not broken why fix it – 1 point;
c. I know I should, but I do not have the drive – 2 points;
d. Continuously and purposefully – 4 points.

Test Results

Up to 5 Points – Opportunities are in your path but you are indifferent to them. You are lazy and lack the right attitude towards seeking or seizing opportunities. Start working on your vigour and your ability to ask questions. All is not lost. Use this book to guide you out of your slumber. Further reading of this book will greatly help to make a difference in your life.

6–10 Points – You fail to recognise the opportunities in your path. Your environment is not conducive to your growth and your goals. Lack of perseverance and diligence to meet opportunities is hindering your success. Your first objective should be to start developing yourself. Improve on your skills and abilities. Do not despair, your help has come in the form of this book. Complete the practical exercises at the end of this chapter and they will help give you insight on how to improve your life.

11–15 Points – You have the potential to meet new opportunities. You have the ability to be efficient and diligent, however you lack perseverance. Pay attention to your environment, look for ways to solve problems. Start by working on yourself; develop yourself by improving your skills, as this will add value to you and subsequently increase your chances of finding opportunities. Pay special attention to the practical assignments at the end of this chapter.

16–20 Points – You have great results! You possess the ability you need to seek and seize opportunities. You have built the right environment for your calling and you are striving to meet opportunities. You do not miss the opportunity to ask questions and you truly manifest perseverance. Share your skills with others!

Practical Assignments

1. **Assess your level of perseverance on a scale of 0 to 10**. What do you lack? List the hindrances preventing you from persistently implementing opportunities. Develop a strategy to combat each item on your list, ensuring it is time bound.

2. **Assess your skills to formulate and ask questions.** What do you need to change in order to gain more chances and opportunities in life?

3. **Write down your plans for self-improvement.** Devote time daily to self-development, define your learning outcome and persist for at least 21 days; if you miss a day you have to start all over again.

4. **How often do you go the "extra mile" on a scale of 0 to 10?** (0 being the least) What disadvantages can you examine in relation to this?

5. **Why should you always do more than is required of you?** Defend this sentence, citing examples from life.

6. **Analyse your surroundings,** asking these questions:

- Who are the people I spend my time with? What kind of people are they?

- How did I develop the relationship I have with the people around me? What do they do for me? What is the essence of our relationship?

- Is my communication with them useful to me? Do I need it?

Once the answers to these questions are established, evaluate the time you spend with your friends. Are you investing your time well? Is it constructive? If not, what do you plan to do about it?

Find a commendable person in your network, ask them to be your mentor and carefully choose a model to follow. Try to find a mentor you will be able to emulate. To do this, analyse the following requirements:

1. Does this role model have followers? This question refers to trust. If a person has no followers, they may not be worth following.

2. What is the strength of your chosen role model, what impact do they have on their followers? What can this person offer you? What is his/her most important advantage?

3. Note: prominent people have both strengths and weaknesses. You do not want to emulate someone else's weaknesses!

4. It is not just about what you can gain from your mentor, every individual also has something to give. What can you give as gratitude for others? This does not need to be monetary. List at least 5 different things you can do to help others grow to success.

Chapter 12

HOW TO TAKE ADVANTAGE OF OPPORTUNITIES

Chapter 12
HOW TO TAKE
ADVANTAGE
OF OPPORTUNITIES

In the previous chapter we discussed the qualities required to recognise and seize opportunities. In this final chapter we will examine the question of how to take advantage of the opportunities that come your way.

– Mum, I'm hungry!

– Okay, pour yourself some soup.

– I don't want soup!

– Then you can warm yourself some pancakes.

– I don't want pancakes either…

– Anything else needs to be cooked, why don't you make yourself some salad?

– I don't want to cut anything. Give me ice cream!

Attention, here is a question! How many more times does the child have to refuse the offer of real food before the mother stops offering options? Most likely not that much longer. It is unlikely the little whiner will get ice cream, and probably not the soup or pancakes either. What does this mean? It is correct to say that, in fact, he is not hungry. This is how we are most times so we miss opportunities.

We say "I want to earn more money" but refuse to invest time in up-skilling to apply for a better role. You justify your lethargy by convincing yourself that you are not in a hurry. You find one excuse or the other, children, family, distance, health, money, environment, lack of opportunity, race, weight, height and so on. We dream of a wonderful relationship, like in a fairy tale, but take no action to cultivate the character required for a healthy relationship.

Is it any wonder that over time, opportunities to realise your goals rarely surface? Analyse your life. Have you been missing opportunities because you are indecisive and lazy?

So how do you take advantage of opportunities?

- Learn to say yes and be true to your word.

- Act immediately, don't leave for tomorrow what you can do today.

- Be aware that opportunities come in the form of small seeds, don't despise the days of small beginnings

- Remember every action has its reward. Choose wisely.

- Do not delay doing things, leave enough time before the deadline. Last minute work is rarely your best work.

- Be able to "unpack" the possibility. Feel the fear and do it anyway.

- Do not wait for a more favourable time, such a time does not exist.

- Do what is inconvenient, that is the essence of growth.

- Be a go-getter, you can do whatever you say you can.

- Look to the future and do what you need to do with integrity in order to achieve all your goals.

Saying Yes to Opportunities is saying Yes to Life

How often do you say no in your life? People often say no even to the smallest and most insignificant

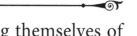

things, fenced off from life, depriving themselves of opportunities and potential gains for a fulfilled life

– Do you want some tea?

– No.

– Let's go to the movies.

– No.

– Will you accept this offer?

– No.

The difference between successful and unsuccessful people is the ability to say yes. Successful people are much more likely to say yes to new ideas as even when they have not assessed how they will execute that idea, they are always willing to take a chance. For example, Richard Branson, British businessman, investor, and philanthropist, is nicknamed "Mr YES" because he responds to all offers with a yes. Optimistic and cheerful people are also more likely to say yes than no, as they are very open to suggestions from friends, relatives and partners. People who find positives in every situation will reap the benefits of opportunities.

The same applies to the area of personal relationships. If one spouse often says no to ideas and proposals from the other half, most likely their union will not be pleasant. However, you will find that if the spouses support each other, positively accepting each other, there is a high degree of happiness in that relationship.

This principle is also relevant to raising children. Too many restrictions cause a child to be fearful of the world around them. Avoid frequent use of the word "No" and other words that denote danger and negativity; so often we unwittingly raise children to believe the world is bad and not likely to improve.

'No' can be expressed in many ways, so beware of the 'no' hidden in 'yes'. When we say 'yes' and add 'but', we negate the yes we spoke.

Here are some examples:

– I would like to do this project, but I'm afraid I will not succeed.

– I'd love to, but I'm in a hurry.

– I would have done it, but I had no time.

– Of course he is not bad, but he has no sense of humour.

Such responses carry a negative charge and also diminish the possibilities in the offering. Be mindful of this type of self-deception, eliminate these combinations of words from your vocabulary and it will open doors to new opportunities in your life.

When you say 'yes', say it firmly with conviction. If you need to say 'no', think carefully so you do not miss an opportunity. We must say 'no' sometimes in order to establish boundaries, but that will not be often. The key to optimum living is to first learn to say 'yes', to be able to grab and implement every opportunity. Then you can say 'no' to demands which do not serve you well to focus on you goals. YES TO OPPORTUNITIES IS YES TO LIFE.

Act Without Delay, take Immediate Action

Taking immediate action is pivotal to success. The art of making a quick decision is key to taking action. Once you agree to do something, do it straight away, and if it is something you cannot do straight away, be determined to do it! In order to be able to take advantage of opportunities, it is important to have the ability to act promptly. As soon as you notice an opportunity, your next step is to take action. Planning, researching, discussing with relevant people are all actions. Anyone who wants to be successful needs to develop these skills; quick decision making and prompt action is the lifeline to opportunities.

"When I decide to do something, I do it quickly," says Carlos Slim, a Mexican businessman of Arab origin, the son of immigrants from Lebanon. TO TEACH YOURSELF to make decisions, begin the process of implementation within 5 seconds. "Leaders have to act more quickly today. The pressure comes much faster," says Andrew Grove, Hungarian-born American businessman, engineer, author and a science pioneer in the semiconductor industry. To be a leader you must learn to act fast.

Remember that Opportunities Come in Forms of Small Seeds -don't despise the days of small beginning

OPPORTUNITIES RARELY COME IN GREAT QUANTITIES. As small as seeds are, when planted on fertile ground the fruit or plant always grow bigger than the seed. Even though the seed is growing, you will not see the growth but be assured it is growing. Another interesting fact using the analogy of seeds: the end product never looks like the seed. Take tomato seeds for example: the tomatoes that grow from planting the seeds look nothing like the seeds.

Another observation from seeds is that the seed must be planted for some time to produce the fruit. The appropriate care and conditions are catalysts to this growth; irrigation, fertiliser and sunlight are all essential. This means that even when nothing is visible on the surface, deep in the soil the seed is germinating from the roots. Only after these processes and time lapse then the sprouts appear on the surface. Sometimes it does not matter if you can't see the process: your ability to see the process of seeds growing will not stop the process or diminish the outcome, but still produces results with time.

Big things usually start small, so we must be able to trust even the smallest of opportunities as potential for growth. Our responsibility is to multiply and convert opportunities to achieve reality in the form of products or a function for society. Be diligent and meticulous – seize the opportunities hidden in small seeds.

Another example of this principle is in conception. When a woman is pregnant she and others may not know until time has passed; it could be weeks from conception before any symptoms or signs of pregnancy begin to show. It is also evident with babies: it is impossible for a baby to be born an adult size – every human being comes into the world small, but it does not mean they will remain small; growth happens even if you cannot see it happening with your naked eyes.

Starting small is good. A pitcher is filled gradually, drop by drop. Each artist was once an amateur. We all start small; do not neglect the small. "Do not despise these small beginnings," Zechariah 4:10. If you are consistent and patient, you will succeed! "Small daily improvements are the key to staggering long-term results," says Robin Sharma, a Canadian writer and one of the most famous North American experts on motivation, leadership and personality development.

Never Leave for Tomorrow Things You Could Accomplish Today

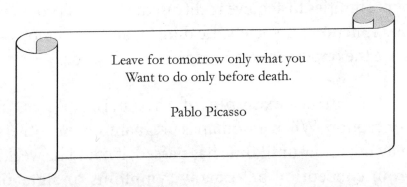

Leave for tomorrow only what you
Want to do only before death.

Pablo Picasso

Ninety-seven per cent of people live with the mind-set of leaving things for tomorrow. The habit of putting off until tomorrow is a damaging habit and leads to loss of opportunities.

When the performance of any task is delayed or deferred you are preventing the opportunity presented by that task from yielding. You also stack up tasks and with each new day, a new task comes, and an increasing weight of tasks undone leads to procrastination. As a result of procrastinating, there is no proper result; lost chances and experiences turn to regrets and emotional distress starts to creep in. "Hard work is a cluster of light things you did not do when they had to be done," says John Maxwell, American author and motivational speaker.

"Your future is created by what you do today, not what you do tomorrow," says Robert Kiyosaki, an American businessman, investor, self-help author, educator, motivational speaker, activist, financial commentator and radio personality. Often opportunities and the ability to respond to them are for the taking, and if you don't someone else will. Therefore, you must seize the opportunity now.

The famous French mathematician, engineer, physicist, writer and philosopher Blaise Pascal wrote: "The virtue of man is not measured by his extraordinary feats, but his daily effort." What we do not start today will not be finished tomorrow, so we should never postpone what we can do now. Anyone who 'leaves for later' will never be able to take advantage of opportunities.

Do Not Leave Things until the Last Minute

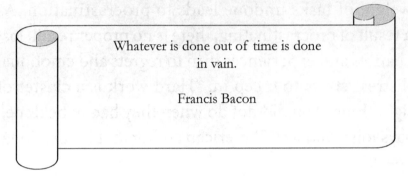

Whatever is done out of time is done
in vain.

Francis Bacon

The habit of putting things off until later is another slayer of opportunities. There are many people with great ideas who never start until they are forgotten. Common in these areas are exercising to improve health, maintaining adequate physical fitness or starting a business – often these good intentions die without finding opportunities. Day after day we put off what we should start today – do we think that tomorrow will never come? He who postpones until later will procrastinate his whole life!

In order to conquer procrastination, let your life principles be as follows:

- Do what you say you will do

- Finish everything you start

- Use time to your advantage; don't leave what you can do now for tomorrow.

When a person is persistent, intensifies his efforts and invests time productively, he or she is bound to succeed. Success in one area will seal the motivation to develop more ideas and achieve even greater success. Doing what we do well and on time will not only help us grow and achieve success, but will also boost our reputation and give us a competitive edge. "Good artists create, great artists steal, and real artists carry out the order in time," said Steve Jobs, American entrepreneur and co-founder of Apple Inc., who was widely regarded as a pioneer in technology. Conversion of time is vital to success, as what you do with your time will determine the level of your success.

The habit of postponing everything until later is laziness. "Tomorrow is the only day of the year that appeals to a lazy person," said Jimmy Lyons, an American musician. Tomorrow is not promised – make today count so that tomorrow can be meaningful.

Laziness is often the high fence that separates us from being able to seize the opportunities that life offers us, leaving us in the cold and causing us to wallow and languish in want. "There is no worse pain than that experienced by a person who has not attained the desired because of their own laziness," said Will Smith, American actor and hip-hop artist nominated for two Oscar awards, four Golden Globe awards, and the winner of a Grammy. In 2008, he was the highest paid actor in the world.

Then there is the 'Rule of 72 hours'. The first 72 hours when an idea or information comes to light is the best time to make a decision and take action. Studies show that people who take action within the first 72 hours achieve the best results, are most effective and are in the top 3% of the world's influencers and the most successful. "The biggest mistake committed by one is doing nothing, fearing that he is doing too little," said Edmund Burke, an Irish statesman born in Dublin, as well as an author, orator, political theorist and philosopher. You need to develop the habit of doing what you need to do, at the very least starting to engage to move the decision forward within 72 hours. It is better to have time left with nothing to do once you have achieved your goal.

Know How to Take Your Opportunities Out of their Box

Life is a gift from God, but you must learn to unwrap the packaging of this gift. Most people never unravel life. Every day, life provides us with opportunities. Successful people see opportunities in each new day. You must also learn to recognise the opportunity in each day; be assured that even if you cannot see it, the fact remains. Opportunities could be in any of your daily seemingly mundane activities, so search, seek and seize.

There is one hidden mistake we sometimes often make when it comes to opportunity: we predetermine where we think our opportunity should come from. This is usually an obstacle to our vision and ability to identify opportunities. Our openness to how and where opportunity will surface can be likened to faith. The knowledge that opportunity has many facets is invaluable. We must avoid limiting our minds to think that opportunity will only come for us from one area or the other. You can find opportunity in any crevice or corner; the universe is creative and we should be too. Help a friend, a stranger – opportunities are hiding where and with whom we might least expect to find them, in the things we do selflessly.

Thomas Edison, American inventor and entrepreneur, very accurately said: "The opportunity is missed by most people because it is dressed ordinarily and looks like work." Take comfort in the benefits to be derived from effort.

Never Wait for a More Comfortable Time

Construct your determination with Sustained Effort, Controlled Attention, and Concentrated Energy. Opportunities never come to those who wait… they are captured by those who dare to attack.

Paul J. Meyer

Lucky people tend to do what
The failures do not like to do. Lucky people
Also do not necessarily like to do it,
But they are subordinate to the feelings of their
task.

E. M. Gray

Waiting for the ideal conditions to carry out your plans is a fallacy and you may be left with nothing. Opportunities and the chance of success are best attained with timely, swift action; it is an illusion to believe there is a favourable time. If you can conceive it, then you can do it; the provision is already available with the idea, you just need to seek it out. "If my mind can conceive it, and my heart can believe it – then I can achieve it," said Muhammad Ali, American Olympic and professional boxer and activist. He is widely regarded as one of the most significant and celebrated sports figures of the 20th century. There will never be a 100% perfect time! People who are waiting for a better time are allowing fortune to pass them by. "Great things need to be done, and not endlessly thought over," said Gaius Julius Caesar, ancient Roman statesman and politician, dictator, commander and writer. The key to seizing the moment lies in doing what is possible in your power to establish momentum and being prepared to make the effort under current conditions.

"Do what you can, what you want and right there where you are," said Theodore Roosevelt American politician, 26th president of the United States and Nobel Peace Prize winner.

Do What Discomforts you, Get Out of your Comfort Zone

Comfort zones are killers. You may still be alive under its delusion, but don't be fooled – if you continue to live under its spell it will definitely kill your dreams. Discipline is needed so that when you are confronted with what you want the most and what you want right now, you will always choose the former. Successful people do what they are uncomfortable with, and do it well. They are able to subject themselves through determination and discipline, converting "I don't want to" into "I can", transforming doubt into possibility. True strength is not found in physical stamina, but in the courage you have to find in giving up the mediocre for purpose. "Strength and growth come only through continuous effort and struggle," said Napoleon Hill, American author and impresario and an early producer of personal-success literature.

It is when you do something despite the "can't", when you gather strength in pain and from distress – this is when the magic of growth happens. If you are not doing things that cause you every effort you can possible give, it is impossible to improve; success always demands more than you are willing to give. When you feel you have given everything you have but keep going, there is an opportunity to create – giving up must never be an option.

You are already born with the ability to be great; to experience your greatness in reality it is necessary to do the extraordinary to achieve the success innate in you.

Do not live in delusions, as anything of value in life is born out of effort. Bill Gates, the inventor of Microsoft, spent months in isolation writing programming language before Microsoft was born. Mark Zuckerberg and friends painstakingly worked on writing the code for Facebook, devoting all their time to it. After launching the social network, Mark continued to work hard for several more years to develop the platform.

Evidently, it is more likely that a person who has taught himself to do what he is uncomfortable doing, what demands painful effort, to gain strength and seize advantage of opportunities. "Things may come to those who wait, but only the things left by those who hustle," said Abraham Lincoln, the 16th President of the United States.

Finish Everything You Start; Do Not Leave Any Task Uncompleted

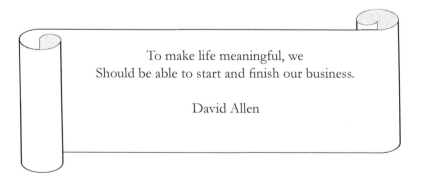

To make life meaningful, we
Should be able to start and finish our business.

David Allen

You should know by now that one complete idea is a lot better than 100 ideas started and abandoned.

Procrastination is the locust of dreams. Knowing the true value of time means seizing and enduring every moment until it is converted to achieve your goal. No idleness, no laziness and no procrastination. Putting off till tomorrow what you can do today is laziness and will often develop into procrastination. There is the story of a person who wanted to drink a cup of tea. He went to make the tea, turned the kettle on to boil the water. He then thought, it is going to take some time for the water to boil and the tea to brew so he switched off the kettle to stop the water from boiling. An hour later he was still craving the tea, so he started the process again. He switched on the kettle to boil water, but as the water was coming to the boil he realised he had no sugar, so he switched off the kettle again. He then went out for sugar and returned an hour later. He put the kettle on again and just before the water boiled he turned off the kettle to answer his phone. After 30 minutes of talking on the phone, he remembered that he was going to make tea, but by this time he had to leave the house and the desire for the tea had gone.

Let us review the time spent. Two times three minutes of switching the kettle on to boil water and turning it off just before it boils. One hour to return from going to get sugar. Thirty minutes of talking on the phone before he realised he had no more time. All of this came to NOTHING. The moral of this story is to focus on our efforts in order to achieve success.

Those who follow through are sure to enjoy the advantage of opportunities. Avoid distractions, focus on your plans. Acquire the skills you need to achieve your goals and persist until you achieve success.

When you are continuously working towards your goals your subconscious mind is engaged and working around the clock attracting the people and circumstances required to achieve success. "Sage is constant as the sun. Fool changes like the moon," wrote Seneca, the Roman Stoic philosopher, poet and statesman, tutor of Nero and one of the leading representatives of Stoicism.

Be Ambitious and Diligent

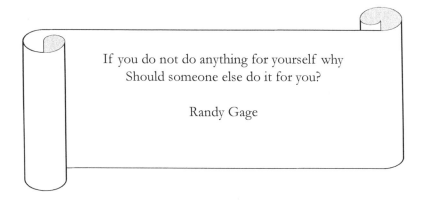

If you do not do anything for yourself why
Should someone else do it for you?

Randy Gage

To reach the top of the ladder you must be determined. Ambition alone will not achieve success, you also need to work diligently towards your goal.

"Character cannot be developed in ease and quiet. Only through experience of trial and tribulation can the soul be strengthened, ambition inspired and success achieved," said Helen Keller, American author, political activist and lecturer. She was the first deaf-blind person to earn a Bachelor of Arts degree.

According to the English dictionary, "ambition is a strong desire and determination to achieve success". It is a catalyst and foundation for success. It also contributes to the formation of leadership qualities which are prevalent in most successful people.

Determination is one of the predictors of success; you must direct it to a goal and turn it into an obsession until it becomes a success. In order to achieve all that we aspire to, we need determination; the value of determination is the achievement. Ambitious people who are diligent and focused find the opportunities they need to achieve their goals.

There are many ways a determined person seizes opportunity. Raising your hand to respond to a question in front of the class, accepting a task that many have declined or taking a voluntary position in the area of your passion are a few characteristics prevalent in ambitious people. When you leave your comfort zone, go where you have never been and start doing things you have never done – you get to learn something new and develop new strengths. The right actions give you the platform to be seen and engaged with other like-minded people. The more you work, the more your chances of opportunity and the more you achieve.

Look Onward to the Future

Among the many inventions of Edison perhaps the most important and overlooked was his laboratory in Menlo Park. It was the first in the history of such a centre, designed for large-scale scientific and research work, the prototype for what would later be called a "think tank". A think tank is now well established as a research institute or an organisation that performs research and advocacy, concerning topics such as social policy, political strategy, and economics, the military, technology and culture. Edison's work in this area set the pace for times to come.

Edison was different because of his many unique talents; his ability to see into the future was a dominant feature of his success. He had insight into the development of technology and of the industry to which he was committed. As a visionary, he created the conditions to support his work then bring about change for the future. "We cannot seek achievement for ourselves and forget about progress and prosperity for our community. Our ambitions must be broad enough to include the aspirations and needs of others, for their sakes and for our own," said Cesar Chavez, an American labour leader and civil rights activist who, with Dolores Huerta, co-founded the National Farm Workers Association in 1962. Similarly, Edison didn't seek to serve only himself in any of his inventions; as a visionary he sought opportunities and created solutions for the benefit of the world, then and in the future.

Lessons from Edison's life and career are to be the solution or develop a solution. Leave a legacy that will outlive you and be of benefit to the world. All that is real is temporary. Scripture asserts that what is visible today is temporary, as the eternal is just what is not yet visible to our eyes (2 Corinthians, 4:18).

Here are some suggestions to kick start your ambition trail. If you are already fluent in English, learn another language – you never know, it could open the door to opportunities for you. Further your education formally or informally through self-development, maybe even outside of the country you reside in now; venture out to other countries as the world is one big community.

Develop foresight in the area of your passion or vocation. The ability to predict and plan for the future is important to advancement in any sphere of life. Vision is a quality possessed by those who have been able to influence and change their world through foresight.

We need to continue to search for opportunities and be the solution for the present as well as the future. Our search for answers is the trigger we need to invite opportunities.

What Plans Do You Have to Change the World for the Better?

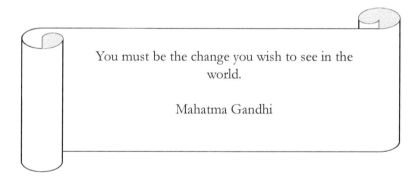

You must be the change you wish to see in the world.

Mahatma Gandhi

The Japanese island of Kashima was once an inhabited colony of wild monkeys, which scientists fed sweet potatoes by throwing them on a floor of sand. The monkeys liked the sweet potato but not the sand on them. One of the monkeys found a way around this problem by washing the sweet potatoes. She taught her mother this trick and the other monkeys followed suit. As the number of monkeys who learned how to wash sweet potatoes reached 100, all the monkeys, who lived on the nearby islands, suddenly, without motive, began to wash their potatoes.

How can this be, you ask? In science, this phenomenon is called the "hundredth monkey effect." This is the effect in which a new behaviour or idea rapidly spreads by unexplained means from one group to all related groups once a critical number of members of the group exhibit the new behaviour or acknowledge the new idea. It happened with all the monkeys in Japan, even with those in the zoos.

As history reveals, all scientific discoveries and achievements take place when the number of researchers reaches a critical mass. Of course, each opening or piece of new information has its own critical mass of people working on it. The "100th Monkey" phenomenon is also true of human endeavours. Perhaps this is very hard to believe, but if you think about it, the thought of just one person has inspired a generation to change many things in our lifetime. The opportunities we seek and seize today could be the phenomenal success of the future. Our goal is to leave an indelible mark for generations to come.

The Whole World depends on the Work Ethic of One Man

Many people underestimate their value and the power of purpose. "Everyone can change the world.

Without it, the 100 becomes just 99. We somehow got used to resignation, and this leads to permissiveness. We have forgotten that one person can do a lot," said Alexander Solzhenitsyn, a Russian writer, poet, activist and Nobel Prize winner for literature.

The world can change all that affects the human consciousness. The question is, who is the world? The simple answer is you and I; however, the answer may also be in the phenomenon "The Butterfly Effect". This is the sensitive dependence on initial conditions in which a small change in one state of a deterministic, nonlinear system can result in large differences in a later state. This concept was presented in a Ray Bradbury short story, "A Sound of Thunder." In the story, a man who arrives in the past on a tour crushes a butterfly, comes back and does not know his reality, so many things have changed. This was confirmed by Nikola Tesla: "The actions of even a tiny creature lead to changes in the entire universe."

We are able to make changes in and around us, to influence the world at large. You have no excuse but to create opportunities and bring your ideas to life! It is important to realise that to help yourself and the world it starts with you and you alone. Life depends on you – you are everything to life. One word, one sentence, one image, one video can change the world – if it touches the hearts of others it will change the world. You can start or stop a war, a revolution or social movement. You can save a life, you can save many lives; you are the world.

Our world today is in need of change. We can change it by realising our dreams. "Your mission on this planet is to reveal your true potential and inspire others with your success; to help rid others of the mediocrity that crippled them," says Randy Gage. This defines the mission of every man. Further reading on this subject can be found in Randy Gage's *Why You Are Dumb, Sick & Broke and How to Become Smart, Healthy And Rich.*

Liberate yourself and your world, so that rather than letting your life become a consequence of other people's choices, you can make a choice for your life. Life is predictable: you can decide what will happen and who you will become, and from the moment you start to make your own decisions to effect changes in your life, the whole universe will give way to you. It will release all the fortune you need as you work to achieve your goals.

Golden Nuggets

1. In the fateful moments of life you need to say "YES."

2. Make a decision and act quickly.

3. Opportunities rarely come big. Look out for the small fortunes.

4. The task, which we do not start today, cannot be completed tomorrow.

5. He who leaves a task for later misses the opportunities of now.

6. Opportunities are missed by most people; they are disguised in work.

7. While waiting for the ideal conditions to carry out the plans, you may be left with nothing.

8. Opportunities come to the one who taught himself to do what is inconvenient.

9. One idea successfully implemented is better than 100 ideas abandoned.

10. When you continuously work towards your goals, the subconscious is working around the clock, attracting people and circumstances that are required for you to achieve the goal.

11. We all depend on you; the power to change the world is in you.

Self-Examination Test

Choose the option that best fits your opinion.

1. Is it better to regret what was done than what has not been done?
a. I do not know – 0 points;
b. No – 1 point;
c. Sometimes – 3 points;
d. Yes – 4 points.

2. How fast do you make decisions?
a. I find it hard to make decisions – 0 points;
b. I rarely make decisions – 1 point;
c. If I have to, I can make a decision fairly quickly – 3 points;
d. I always make decisions quickly – 4 points.

3. How often do you complete any task?
c. Rarely, no time – 0 points;
d. I do what I can – 1 point;
e. Most of the time – 2 points;
f. I sort things according to their priority and finish each in due time – 4 points.

4. What is your attitude towards your work?

d. I can do better – 0 points;

e. I get solace on my days off – 1 point;

f. My feelings are secondary, I do my duty well and rest in my spare time – 2 points;

g. I am fulfilled in my job and I work hard to improve daily – 4 points.

5. If 100 people had to speak at an event, when would you be taking the stage to speak?

e. I would not put myself in that situation – 0 points;

f. Somewhere among the last group of people – 1 point;

g. I would like a position in the middle – 2 points;

h. I would be among the first to speak – 4 points.

Test Results

Up to 6 Points – You urgently need to make changes in your life. Your ability to organise yourself is at ground zero. It is strongly recommended that you carefully work through this book and begin to apply all the principles set out herein.

7–11 Points – You are not seizing the opportunities as they come your way. Your lack of interest is destructive. You have to take your life in your hands and begin to set goals and take action to achieve success. The advice contained in this book will help you if you start to put them into practice.

12–16 Points – You know what to do and you are able to prioritise. However, you seem to be lacking some key skills to success. The path to success is not closed, all it takes is you believing in yourself and focusing on actions to achieve your goals.

17–20 Points – Congratulations! You have excellent skills in managing your own affairs. Practically, you are an expert in this area! Help others to develop as well as you have and the reward is more strength and opportunities opening for you.

Practical Assignments

1. Take a look at your life: what areas are you not satisfied with, what would you like to improve? Think of all the offers of help that come to you and how you respond to others who seek your support. Complete an action plan from the list of your dissatisfactions, be specific and give yourself deadlines to complete the actions.

2. In your own words, what is the benefit of making a decision quickly and following through without delay?

3. In your opinion, why do opportunities sometimes come in small doses? If the opportunity looks promising, what does this mean?

4. Putting off until tomorrow what you can do today. What does this statement mean to you and how does it inform your ability to seize opportunities?

5. Thomas Edison: "Opportunities are missed by most people because they are dressed ordinarily and look like work"? What does this statement mean to you? What conclusions do you make on the basis of your life in light of the areas covered in this book?

6. Why is it not necessary to wait until a favourable time or condition before you take action?

7. Successful people do what is uncomfortable and what they do not like to do. What would a person with a mediocre attitude to life do in the same situation? Explain your answer.

8. Always consider the future and prepare for tomorrow. Create a plan for the next five years. This must include key areas of your life.

9. Why is it important to be determined? What advantages does it give? What are you missing when

you are not determined? What are your plans to develop this trait?

10. What decisions have you made to improve your life and multiply your efforts in seeking and seizing opportunities after reading this book? What changes are you going to implement immediately? What plans do you have for your community or the world at large?

CONCLUSION

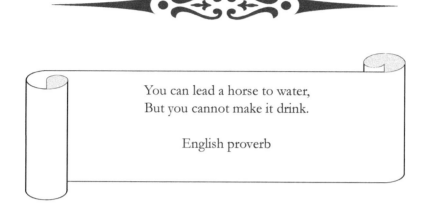

You can lead a horse to water,
But you cannot make it drink.

English proverb

Dear Reader,

This is the end of our journey through understanding that life is an opportunity. We have walked through the vastness of POSSIBILITIES. The fact that you have read this book to the end shows that you now possess an incomparably greater knowledge than before. I encourage you to read it again and again until the lessons of this book become innate in you. I also challenge you with greater urgency to pay attention to the opportunities all around you.

Finally, an idiom to aid your understanding. A senior professor assigned some students to his trainee. The trainee, a competent young man, thought about all his classes with diligence, ensuring all the students assigned to him understood the subject. On reflection, he went back to his senior professor, concerned that none of his students were applying the lessons. The senior instructor was wise. He instructed his trainee to prepare a horse for the lake.

Early in the morning they embarked on the journey. The road was not too difficult, although it still took them some time. Three hours later they arrived at a lake.

The professor asked the trainee to bring him some water, and also take the horse to drink some water. The trainee ran the errands, and they sat down under a big tree for a picnic. As soon as they finished eating, the professor asked the trainee: "Now the horse needs a little more to drink, take him to the lake, please." The trainee had a few doubts, but still led the horse to the lake. The horse stood at the lake without making any attempt to drink. The trainee took the horse back to the professor. "Professor, I have done as instructed, but the horse refused to drink." The teacher was not surprised and nodded in acceptance.

They sat and enjoyed the wonderful view and the singing birds. Half an hour passed. The professor asked the trainee to take the horse to the lake for water again.

The trainee politely followed the instructions of his professor. History repeated itself, the horse did not want to drink. The trainee stood a little longer before returning to the professor with the horse. Again, the trainee said to his professor, "the horse did not want to drink". The professor asked him several times to take the horse to the lake, and the result was the same. Several times the teacher asked the trainee to try to tilt the muzzle of the horse directly to the water.

Finally, the professor said, "You see, you can lead a horse to drink water and even direct her face to the water, but you cannot make it drink. In the end, only she decides when to drink. There will come a time when the horse (analogy for people) will experience a thirst for knowledge, and accept the offer presented to him or her." The trainee thanked his teacher for his wise counsel.

"You can lead a horse to water but you can't make him drink" is a proverb which means that you can give someone an opportunity but not force them to take it. Many people can bring opportunities right to our doorstep, but still refuse to make use of them. Opportunities are accepted and converted to achievement by those who really want it. Each of us will be provided a life worthy and full of chances. For each of us, life will lead us to be watered under great waterfalls, but the choice to drink is up to us. It all depends on our individual choices. Life truly is a source full of new opportunities.

"Don't cry over the shots you've missed; weep over the ones you've not taken at all. The bitterest regrets are for things planned but left undone."

Israelmore Ayivor

THE END!

SUNDAY ADELAJA'S
BIOGRAPHY

Pastor Sunday Adelaja is the Founder and Senior Pastor of The Embassy of the Blessed Kingdom of God for All Nations Church in Kyiv, Ukraine.

Sunday Adelaja is a Nigerian-born Leader, Thinker, Philosopher, Transformation Strategist, Pastor, Author and Innovator who lives in Kiev, Ukraine.

At 19, he won a scholarship to study in the former Soviet Union. He completed his master's program in Belorussia State University with distinction in journalism.

At 33, he had built the largest evangelical church in Europe — The Embassy of the Blessed Kingdom of God for All Nations.

Sunday Adelaja is one of the few individuals in our world who has been privileged to speak in the United Nations, Israeli Parliament, Japanese Parliament and the United States Senate.

The movement he pioneered has been instrumental in reshaping lives of people in the Ukraine, Russia and about 50 other nations where he has his branches.

His congregation, which consists of ninety-nine percent white Europeans, is a cross-cultural model of the church for the 21st century.

His life mission is to advance the Kingdom of God on earth by raising a generation of history makers who will live for a cause larger, bigger and greater than themselves. Those who will live like Jesus and transform every sphere of the society in every nation as a model of the Kingdom of God on earth.

His economic empowerment program has succeeded in raising over 200 millionaires in the short period of three years.

Sunday Adelaja is the author of over 300 books, many of which are translated into several languages including Russian, English, French, Chinese, German, etc.

His work has been widely reported by world media outlets such as The Washington Post, The Wall Street Journal, New York Times, Forbes, Associated Press, Reuters, CNN, BBC, German, Dutch and French national television stations.

Pastor Sunday is happily married to his "Princess" Bose Dere-Adelaja. They are blessed with three children: Perez, Zoe and Pearl.

Bill Clinton —
42Nd President Of The
United States (1993–2001),
Former Arcansas State
Governor

Ariel "Arik" Sharon —
Israeli Politician, Israeli
Prime Minister (2001–2006)

Benjamin Netanyahu —
Statesman Of Israel. Israeli
Prime Minister (1996–1999),
Acting Prime Minister
(From 2009)

Jean ChrEtien —
Canadian Politician,
20Th Prime Minister Of
Canada, Minister Of Justice
Of Canada, Head Of Liberan
Party Of Canada

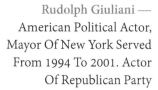

Rudolph Giuliani —
American Political Actor,
Mayor Of New York Served
From 1994 To 2001. Actor
Of Republican Party

Colin Powell —
Is An American Statesman
And A Retired Four-Star
General In The Us Army,
65Th United States Secretary
Of State

Peter J. Daniels —
Is A Well-Known And
Respected Australian
Christian International
Business Statesman Of
Substance

Madeleine
Korbel Albright —
An American Politician And
Diplomat, 64Th United States
Secretary Of State

Kenneth Robert
Livingstone —
An English Politician,
1St Mayor Of London
(4 May 2000 – 4 May
2008), Labour Party
Representative

Sir Richard Charles Nicholas Branson —
English Business Magnate, Investor And Philanthropist. He Founded The *Virgin Group,* Which Controls More Than 400 Companies

Mel Gibson —
American Actor And Filmmaker

Chuck Norris —
American Martial Artist, Actor, Film Producer And Screenwriter

Christopher Tucker —
American Actor
And Comedian

Bernice Albertine King —
American Minister Best
Known As The Youngest
Child Of Civil Rights Leaders
Martin Luther King Jr. And
Coretta Scott King Andrew

Andrew Young — American
Politician, Diplomat, And
Activist, 14[Th] United States
Ambassador To The United
Nations, 55[Th] Mayor Of
Atlanta

General Wesley
Kanne Clark —
4-Star General And Nato
Supreme Allied Commander

Dr. Sunday Adelaja's family:
Perez, Pearl, Zoe and Pastor Bose Adelaja

FOLLOW
SUNDAY ADELAJA
ON SOCIAL MEDIA

Subscribe And Read Pastor Sunday's Blog:
www.sundayadelajablog.com

**Follow these links and listen to over 200
of Pastor Sunday`s Messages free of charge:**
http://sundayadelajablog.com/content/

Follow Pastor Sunday on Twitter:
www.twitter.com/official_pastor

**Join Pastor Sunday's Facebook
page to stay in touch:**
www.facebook.com/
pastor.sunday.adelaja

**Visit our websites for more
information about Pastor
Sunday's ministry:**
http://www.godembassy.com
http://www.
pastorsunday.com
http://sundayadelaja.de

CONTACT

USA
CORNERSTONE PUBLISHING
info@thecornerstonepublishers.com
+1 (516) 547-4999
www.thecornerstonepublishers.com

AFRICA
SUNDAY ADELAJA MEDIA LTD.
E-mail: btawolana@hotmail.com
+2348187518530, +2348097721451, +2348034093699

LONDON, UK
PASTOR ABRAHAM GREAT
abrahamagreat@gmail.com
+447711399828, +441908538141

KIEV, UKRAINE
pa@godembassy.org
Mobile: +380674401958

Best Selling Books by Dr. Sunday Adelaja
Available on Amazon.com and Okadabooks.com

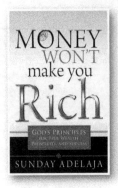
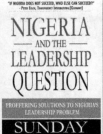

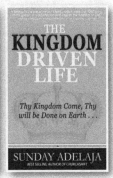

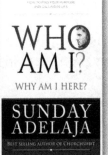

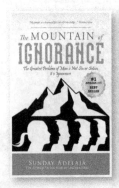

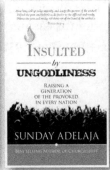
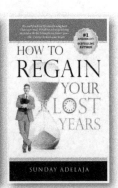

Best Selling Books by Dr. Sunday Adelaja
Available on Amazon.com and Okadabooks.com

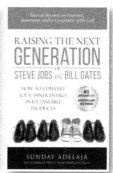
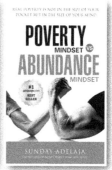

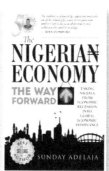
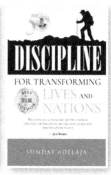

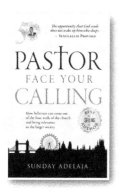

FOR DISTRIBUTION OR TO ORDER BULK COPIES OF THIS BOOKS, PLEASE CONTACT US:

USA | CORNERSTONE PUBLISHING
E-mail: info@thecornerstonepublishers.com, +1 (516) 547-4999
www.thecornerstonepublishers.com

AFRICA | SUNDAY ADELAJA MEDIA LTD.
E-mail: btawolana@hotmail.com
+2348187518530, +2348097721451, +2348034093699

LONDON, UK | PASTOR ABRAHAM GREAT
E-mail: abrahamagreat@gmail.com, +447711399828, +441908538141

KIEV, UKRAINE |
E-mail: pa@godembassy.org, Mobile: +380674401958

GOLDEN JUBILEE SERIES BOOKS
BY DR. SUNDAY ADELAJA

FOR DISTRIBUTION OR TO ORDER BULK COPIES OF THIS BOOKS, PLEASE CONTACT US:

USA | CORNERSTONE PUBLISHING
E-mail: info@thecornerstonepublishers.com, +1 (516) 547-4999
www.thecornerstonepublishers.com

AFRICA | SUNDAY ADELAJA MEDIA LTD.
E-mail: btawolana@hotmail.com
+2348187518530, +2348097721451, +2348034093699

LONDON, UK | PASTOR ABRAHAM GREAT
E-mail: abrahamagreat@gmail.com, +447711399828, +441908538141

KIEV, UKRAINE |
E-mail: pa@godembassy.org, Mobile: +380674401958

CPSIA information can be obtained
at www.ICGtesting.com
Printed in the USA
LVHW080152160720
660826LV00015B/217